Learning System Center App Controller

Design, implement, and manage System Center App Controller

Nasir Naeem

BIRMINGHAM - MUMBAI

Learning System Center App Controller

First published: February 2015

Production reference: 1180215

Published by Packt Publishing Ltd.
Livery Place
35 Livery Street
Birmingham B3 2PB, UK.

ISBN 978-1-78439-853-8

www.packtpub.com

Credits

Author
Nasir Naeem

Reviewers
Florian Klaffenbach
Anderson Patricio
Lai Yoong Seng

Commissioning Editor
Dipika Gaonkar

Acquisition Editors
Richard Gall
James Jones

Content Development Editor
Ruchita Bhansali

Technical Editors
Rosmy George
Ankita Thakur

Copy Editors
Pranjali Chury
Vikrant Phadke

Project Coordinator
Nidhi Joshi

Proofreaders
Ting Baker
Simran Bhogal

Indexer
Rekha Nair

Production Coordinator
Alwin Roy

Cover Work
Alwin Roy

About the Author

Nasir Naeem lives in Birmingham, England. He works for Inframon as a system center consultant. He has been working in the IT field for just over a decade, mostly working on Windows-based networks with a combination of Cisco as well as VMWare.

When not working with clients to improve IT cost efficiency and administration improvements, he is an Arduino electronics hobbyist.

Writing a book is a huge task and this book is no exception. This book is dedicated to my parents and teachers; their debt I cannot pay back.

Over the years, many people have provided guidance and helped steer the direction of my career. Some of the prominent names are Chris Page (WCC), Alwyn Wayne (WCC), Paul Hewitt (IBM), Alexandra Webb (WCC), Paul Forkgen (NAK Group), and John Parker (NAK Group). Also, sincere thanks to Richard Gall for providing an opportunity to write this book.

About the Reviewers

Florian Klaffenbach started his IT career in 2004 as a first and second level IT support technician and IT salesman trainee for a B2B online shop. After that, he moved to a small company working as an IT project manager, planning, implementing, and integrating from industrial plants and laundries into IT enterprise. After spending some years as an IT project manager, he moved to Dell Germany. Here, he started from scratch as an enterprise technical support analyst and later worked on a project to start Dell technical communities and support over social media in Europe and outside of the U.S. Currently, he is working as a solutions architect and consultant for Microsoft infrastructure and cloud specializing in Microsoft Hyper-V, file services, System Center Virtual Machine Manager, and Microsoft Azure IaaS.

In addition to his job, he is active as a Microsoft blogger and lecturer. He blogs, for example, on his own page, Datacenter-Flo.de, or the Brocade Germany community. Together with a very good friend, he founded the Windows Server User Group Berlin to create a network of Microsoft IT professionals in Berlin. Florian maintains a very tight network for many vendors, such as Cisco, Dell, or Microsoft, and other communities. This helps him grow his experience and get the best out of a solution for his customers.

Florian has worked for several companies such as Dell Germany, CGI Germany, and his first employer, TACK GmbH. Currently, he works for Elanity Network Partner together with Benedict Berger (Microsoft Most Valuable Professional—Hyper-V).

I want to thank Packt Publishing for giving me the chance to review the book and my girlfriend for not killing me because I spent lots of our free time on the review.

Anderson Patricio is a Canadian Exchange Server MVP and a messaging consultant based in Toronto, designing and deploying messaging solutions for several clients located in America. He has been working with the Exchange Server since Version 5 and besides his passion with Exchange Server, he works with Active Directory and System Center products.

Anderson is an active member of the Exchange Community and he contributes to forums, blogs, tutorials, articles, and videos. In English, he blogs regularly at `www.AndersonPatricio.ca` and `MSExchange.org`, where he writes his blog and articles. In Portuguese, his website (`www.AndersonPatricio.org`) contains hundreds of Microsoft articles that help the local community. Besides this, he is also involved in speaking engagements; he is a TechEd speaker in South America and is part of Microsoft Virtual Academy (MVA) training courses. You can also follow him on Twitter at `http://twitter.com/apatricio`.

He is the reviewer of several books such as *Windows Powershell in Action, Bruce Payette, PowerShell in Practice, Richard Siddaway*, both by Manning Publication, and *Microsoft Exchange 2010 PowerShell Cookbook* by *Mike Pfeiffer, Packt Publishing*.

Lai Yoong Seng was awarded Microsoft Most Valuable Professional (MVP) for Hyper-V in 2010. He has more than 14 years of IT experience and recently joined Hyper-V and System Center Specialist Infront Consulting in Malaysia. He specializes in Microsoft virtualization, blogs about the technology (`www.ms4u.info`), and has presented at local and regional events. He is the founder of Malaysia Virtualization User Group (MVUG), which provides a one-stop center for people to learn about Hyper-V, System Center, and Azure. Previously, he was actively engaged in the Technology Adoption Program (TAP) and was a tester for System Center Virtual Machine Manager 2012, System Center 2012 SP1, Windows Server 2012 R2, System Center 2012 R2, and Azure Site Recovery. Besides this, he has been a technical reviewer for *Windows Server 2012 Hyper-V: Deploying Hyper-V Enterprise Server Virtualization Platform, Hyper-V Network Virtualization Cookbook,* and *Hyper-V Security,* all by Packt Publishing, and also for a video *Building and Managing a Virtual Environment with Hyper-V Server 2012 R2, Packt Publishing.*

Reviewing a book takes a lot of effort, process, and determination. It would not have been possible without help from family, colleagues, and friends. I would like to thank my parents for being understanding, patient, and helping me keep it all together while I was reviewing a book.

Finally, a very special thanks to Packt Publishing for giving me an opportunity to contribute to this book.

www.PacktPub.com

Support files, eBooks, discount offers, and more

For support files and downloads related to your book, please visit www.PacktPub.com.

Did you know that Packt offers eBook versions of every book published, with PDF and ePub files available? You can upgrade to the eBook version at www.PacktPub.com and as a print book customer, you are entitled to a discount on the eBook copy. Get in touch with us at service@packtpub.com for more details.

At www.PacktPub.com, you can also read a collection of free technical articles, sign up for a range of free newsletters and receive exclusive discounts and offers on Packt books and eBooks.

https://www2.packtpub.com/books/subscription/packtlib

Do you need instant solutions to your IT questions? PacktLib is Packt's online digital book library. Here, you can search, access, and read Packt's entire library of books.

Why subscribe?

- Fully searchable across every book published by Packt
- Copy and paste, print, and bookmark content
- On demand and accessible via a web browser

Free access for Packt account holders

If you have an account with Packt at www.PacktPub.com, you can use this to access PacktLib today and view 9 entirely free books. Simply use your login credentials for immediate access.

Instant updates on new Packt books

Get notified! Find out when new books are published by following @PacktEnterprise on Twitter or the *Packt Enterprise* Facebook page.

Table of Contents

Preface

This book has been written specifically for IT professionals who need to learn System Center App Controller quickly. In this book, you will find chapters separated by topics that are task-specific, intentionally utilizing the minimum amount of theoretical jargon and providing step-by-step information to complete the task successfully. We hope you will enjoy this book as much as we enjoyed writing it for you.

What this book covers

Chapter 1, Introduction to System Center 2012 R2 App Controller, provides an introduction and outlines setting up App Controller, prerequisites, issues addressed by App Controller, a planning guide, and common issues to keep in mind during planning and deployment phases.

Chapter 2, Installing and Working with Different App Controller Components, provides step-by-step instructions for the installation of SQL Server, the installation of required services, and then deployment of System Center App Controller Server.

Chapter 3, Deploying and Configuring System Center Virtual Machine Manager Server, provides step-by-step instructions for completing a successful installation of SCVMM 2012 R2 Server. After completing the installation, further instructions are provided to create a private cloud.

Chapter 4, Customizing App Controller, introduces you to the App Controller administrative portal. Further instructions are provided to integrate the SCVMM server with App Controller. It also covers integrating the Azure cloud subscription, roles-based access, adding network share to the SCVMM server, and configuring the SSL certificate for the App Controller website.

Chapter 5, *Exploring Advanced Options*, provides some of the common day-to-day tasks faced by IT professionals administering a hybrid private and public cloud network. You will be introduced to the PowerShell module for App Controller, Windows Azure PowerShell module installation, and copying VHD files to the Azure cloud.

Chapter 6, *Backup and Recovery*, introduces you to the choices available for backing up App Controller. It provides step-by-step instructions to back up App Controller.

What you need for this book

To follow exercises in this book, System Center 2012 R2 evaluation for App Controller and Virtual Machine Manager along with the evaluation version of SQL Server 2012 Service Pack 2 and the Windows Server 2012 R2 operating system are required. A virtual or physical server running ADDS services and an evaluation version of Microsoft Azure subscription for completing the Azure connectivity steps is required. Windows Server 2012 R2 Server with Hyper-V role enabled is required to add as a host server in VMM and to boot the virtual machine.

Who this book is for

This book is intended for IT professionals working with Hyper-V, the Azure cloud, VMM, and private cloud technology, looking for a quick way to get up to speed with System Center 2012 R2 App Controllers. VMM administrators will also benefit from this book as it addresses managing Azure subscription with App Controller and moving data from the private cloud to public cloud.

To get the most from this book, you should be familiar with Microsoft Hyper-V technology. Knowledge of Virtual Machine Manager is helpful but not necessary. Access to a physical server or cluster running Windows Server 2012 R2 and Hyper-V extensions enabled is necessary to perform the steps related to Hyper-V.

All of the System Center 2012 R2 Components, including Windows Server 2012 R2, are available as a 180-days trial from Microsoft download center.

Conventions

In this book, you will find a number of text styles that distinguish between different kinds of information. Here are some examples of these styles and an explanation of their meaning.

Code words in text, database table names, folder names, filenames, file extensions, pathnames, dummy URLs, user input, and Twitter handles are shown as follows: "In our case, it is a domain user account created for SQL services that is `srv_sql_acc`."

A block of code is set as follows:

```
Import-Module AppController
$cred= Get-credential
$scac= 'https://appcontroller.contoso.internal'
Get-SCACServer -ServerName $scac -Credential $cred
```

New terms and **important words** are shown in bold. Words that you see on the screen, for example, in menus or dialog boxes, appear in the text like this: "Right-click and select **Run as administrator**."

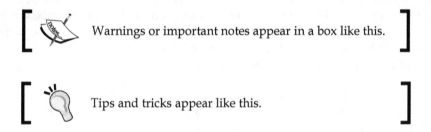

Warnings or important notes appear in a box like this.

Tips and tricks appear like this.

Reader feedback

Feedback from our readers is always welcome. Let us know what you think about this book—what you liked or disliked. Reader feedback is important for us as it helps us develop titles that you will really get the most out of.

To send us general feedback, simply e-mail `feedback@packtpub.com`, and mention the book's title in the subject of your message.

If there is a topic that you have expertise in and you are interested in either writing or contributing to a book, see our author guide at `www.packtpub.com/authors`.

Customer support

Now that you are the proud owner of a Packt book, we have a number of things to help you to get the most from your purchase.

Downloading the color images of this book

We also provide you with a PDF file that has color images of the screenshots/ diagrams used in this book. The color images will help you better understand the changes in the output. You can download this file from: `http://www.packtpub. com/sites/default/files/downloads/8538EN_ColoredImages.pdf`.

Errata

Although we have taken every care to ensure the accuracy of our content, mistakes do happen. If you find a mistake in one of our books—maybe a mistake in the text or the code—we would be grateful if you could report this to us. By doing so, you can save other readers from frustration and help us improve subsequent versions of this book. If you find any errata, please report them by visiting `http://www.packtpub. com/submit-errata`, selecting your book, clicking on the **Errata Submission Form** link, and entering the details of your errata. Once your errata are verified, your submission will be accepted and the errata will be uploaded to our website or added to any list of existing errata under the Errata section of that title.

To view the previously submitted errata, go to `https://www.packtpub.com/books/ content/support` and enter the name of the book in the search field. The required information will appear under the **Errata** section.

Piracy

Piracy of copyrighted material on the Internet is an ongoing problem across all media. At Packt, we take the protection of our copyright and licenses very seriously. If you come across any illegal copies of our works in any form on the Internet, please provide us with the location address or website name immediately so that we can pursue a remedy.

Please contact us at `copyright@packtpub.com` with a link to the suspected pirated material.

We appreciate your help in protecting our authors and our ability to bring you valuable content.

Questions

If you have a problem with any aspect of this book, you can contact us at `questions@packtpub.com`, and we will do our best to address the problem.

1

Introduction to System Center 2012 R2 App Controller

It has been a long journey for the evolution of App Controller. We will be discussing how this component evolved during the last couple of iterations of the VMM product.

App Controller is a component of the System Center family. Historically, it used to be the self-service portal in the Virtual Machine Manager 2008 R2 server. With the release of the System Center 2012 suite, Microsoft consolidated SCCM, SCOM, VMM, SCSM, Orchestrator, Data Protection Manager, and Software Update Publisher (**SUP**) as a single-bundle software suite to manage enterprise data centers. With the release of System Center 2012 Service Pack 1, the system center's virtual machine manager self-service portal was removed from Virtual Machine Manager Server and distributed as System Center App Controller. It was a well-timed change, as Microsoft was addressing its move towards a Cloud OS-centric approach.

To date, System Center App Controller is an extension of Virtual Machine Manager. It adds further functionality to Virtual Machine Manager by exposing role-based access control for users consuming resources allocated in the private cloud, as well as adding functionality to manage public cloud services such as Microsoft Azure.

In this chapter, we will cover the following topics:

- Introduction to App Controller
- Considerations before beginning installation
- Overview of the prerequisites required

Issues addressed by System Center App Controller

With the release of System Center 2012 Service Pack 1, the self-service portal was removed from Virtual Machine Manager and introduced as a separate component of the System Center suite. Up to this point, the private cloud and public cloud were two distinct technologies. To manage a public cloud such as Microsoft Azure, we had to log on to the Microsoft Azure Management portal; and to manage our private cloud, we had to log in to the System Center Virtual Machine Manager. System Center App Controller gave us a single pane where we can manage Windows Azure resources in the cloud, on-premises private cloud management capability, and ability to allow access to resources modelled around business function as a user role, hence simplifying security management and administration of a multi-tenant environment.

Quick planning primer

For planning and design purposes, App Controller is one of the simplest components of the System Center family. To get the App Controller up and running quickly, the Web IIS role is required on at least one of supported server operating systems. A supported SQL Server is required to store the App Controller database. To get extended App Controller features enabled, a component of the System Center family, named Virtual Machine Manager Server, is required in the environment. It can provision, manage, and convert virtual machines. We can also use a shared storage to convert and upload virtual machines to the Microsoft Azure cloud. There is also a requirement of Active Directory Certificates Services if we want to use a certificate from a trusted corporate certification authority, although a self-signed certificate can also be used.

If we want to make App Controller highly available, there are three options possible, as follows:

- Making the database highly available by installing the database on a clustered SQL Server instance
- Making the App Controller server highly available either by creating a virtual machine on a Hyper-V cluster and making the virtual machine highly available or installing multiple App Controller servers behind a load balancer

If multiple App Controller servers are installed behind a load balancer, an encryption key will have to be extracted using the Export-SCACAesKey PowerShell cmdlet. Then you will need to import the extracted key on each load-balanced App Controller server during the installation process.

Installing the prerequisites

Let's cover the prerequisites for successful installation of App Controller. System Center Virtual Machine Manager has to be deployed in the environment to extend App Controller's management capability of administrating a private cloud. App Controller extends Virtual Machine Manager's capabilities and allows conversion and uploads of virtual machines from a private cloud to the public cloud.

Windows assessment and deployment toolkit for Windows 8.1

The Windows ADK toolkit is required in order to install System Center 2012 R2 Virtual Machine Manager Server. Windows Assessment and Deployment Kit is a free toolkit from Microsoft, and can be downloaded from http://www.microsoft.com/en-gb/download/details.aspx?id=39982. It can be installed on the following operating systems:

- Windows 8.1
- Windows 8
- Windows 7
- Windows Sever 2012 R2
- Windows Server 2012
- Windows Server 2008 R2
- Windows Sever 2008
- Windows Vista

Microsoft .NET 4.5 is required for successful installation, and is installed automatically if it is missing. Windows Server 2012 has .NET 4.5 installed out of the box.

Windows Assessment and Deployment Kit for Windows 8.1 includes the following components:

- **Application Compatibility Toolkit (ACT)**: This can be used to build inventories of software installed on computers and also to assess compatibility with Windows 8.1 after migration. This component requires SQL Server 2005 or newer versions. The SQL Server Express edition can also be used.

- **Deployment Tools**: This includes DISM and other deployment tools used to customize disk images and automate deployment.

- **Windows Preinstallation Environment**: This is a small-footprint operating system that can be used to prepare a computer for installation and servicing. It is dependent on Deployment Tools.

- **User State Migration Tool**: This tool is used to migrate user data from one Windows-based machine to another. It includes three packages: ScanState, LoadState, and USMTUtils.

- **Volume Activation Management Tool**: This tool can be used for automatic activation of Windows and Microsoft Office. SQL Server 2008 or a newer version is required to hold the database file.

- **Windows Performance Toolkit**: This tool can be used to monitor application performance against Windows operating system profiles. WPT includes Windows Performance Recorder, Windows Performance Analyzer, and Xperf tools.

- **Windows Assessment Toolkit**: This tool can produce diagnostic and remediation information against a local system by running jobs to measure reliability, performance, and functionality. It requires Deployment Tools, Windows PE, Windows Performance Tools and SQL Server. All of these are included in the ADK 8.1 download.

After downloading the `adksetup.exe` file, the setup process will attempt to download 4 gigabytes of files during the installation process. We can also download the ADK kit for offline usage, and transfer the files to the required server over LAN for easier access. For installation, perform the following steps:

1. To download the files for local access, browse to the location where `adksetup.exe` has been stored. Right-click and select **Run as administrator**, as shown in the following screenshot:

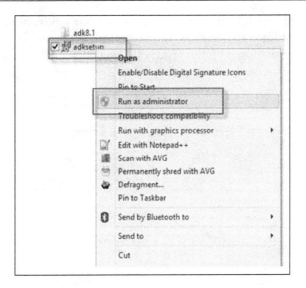

2. After the installation wizard starts, select the **Download the Windows Assessment and Deployment Kit for Windows 8.1 for installation on a separate computer** option. Then specify the download location path under **Download Path**. To keep the installation files isolated, I always create a subfolder in the same location where adksetup.exe is located. Ensure that enough space is available on the disk and then click on **Next**, as shown in this screenshot:

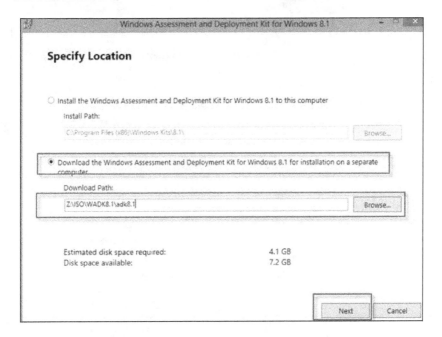

3. Select the appropriate answer according to your environment for **Join the Customer Experience Improvement Program**. It does help Microsoft in creating a better product. Then click on **Next**, as shown in the following screenshot:

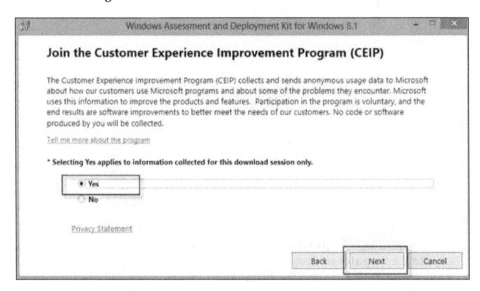

4. Accept the license agreement by clicking on **Accept**, as shown here:

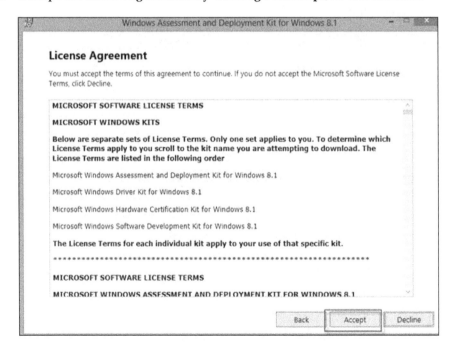

5. After you accept the license agreement, the process of downloading the required files will begin, as shown in the following screenshot:

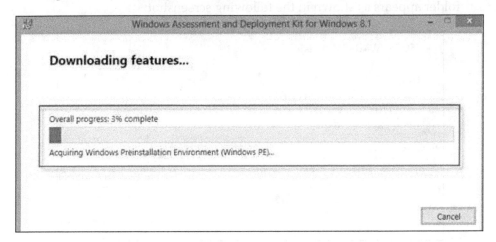

6. Click on **Close** after the download has completed successfully, as shown in this screenshot:

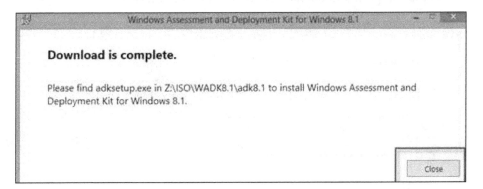

7. Once the download process has been completed, start `adksetup.exe` from the folder where the complete package files have been downloaded. The folder appears as shown in the following screenshot:

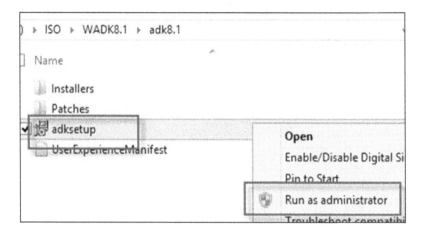

8. This time, the installation options will be slightly different. Select the installation path and click on **Next**, as shown in this screenshot:

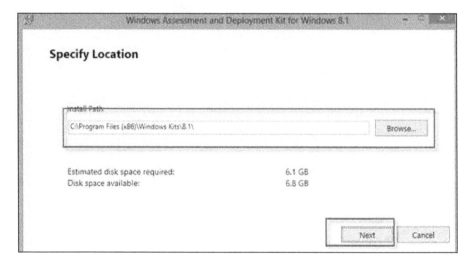

9. Select the appropriate answer according to your organization in the **Join the Customer Experience Improvement Program** section, and click on **Next**, as shown in the following screenshot:

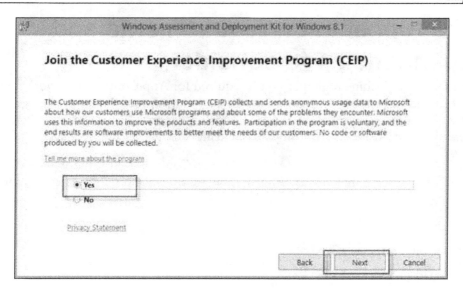

10. Accept the terms and conditions. Then you will be presented with the section about installation of features. Select the **Deployment Tools** and **Windows Preinstallation Environment (Windows PE)** features only, and then click on **Install**, as shown here:

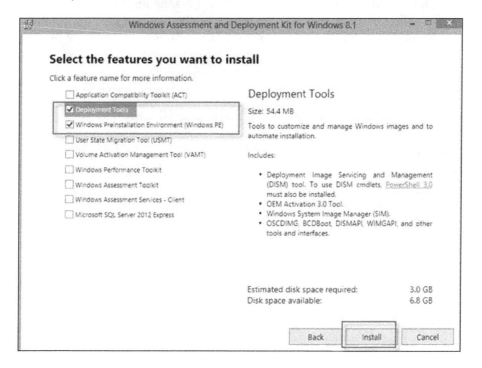

Other application requirements and dependencies to consider

System Virtual Machine Manager is still required for App Controller to work with private cloud resources. For instructions on installing Virtual Machine Manager, refer to the *Installing System Center 2012 R2 Virtual Machine Manager* section in *Chapter 3, Deploying and Configuring System Center Virtual Machine Manager Server*.

We will be installing System Center 2012 R2 App Controller on Windows Server 2012 R2. App Controller's server-side components are supported by Microsoft on the following operating systems:

- Windows Server 2008
- Windows Server 2008 SP2
- Windows Server 2008 R2
- Windows Server 2008 R2 SP 1
- Windows Server 2012 Standard, Datacenter edition
- Windows Server 2012 R2 Standard, Datacenter edition

System Center 2012 R2 Application Controller requires the IIS role installed to function. If the IIS role is not enabled, the setup installer enables the role automatically, with the correct features enabled. The required IIS features are as follows:

- Static Content
- Default Document
- Directory Browsing
- HTTP Errors
- ASP.NET
- .NET Extensibility
- ISAPI Extensions
- ISAPI Filters
- HTTP Logging
- Request Logging
- Tracing
- Basic Authentication
- Windows Authentication

- Request Filtering
- Static Content Compression
- IIS Management Console

Microsoft .NET Framework 4.5 should also be installed. The setup wizard will install .NET 4.5 if it's missing. On Windows Server 2012 R2, .NET Framework 4.5 is installed by default.

The App Controller server must be member of an Active Directory Domain. Besides, Virtual Machine Manager Console needs to be installed as a software requirement on the App Controller server.

System Center 2012 R2 App Controller requires access to a SQL server to store critical data. Microsoft-supported versions of SQL Server for System Center 2012 R2 App Controller are as follows.

- SQL Server 2008 R2 SP2 Standard, Datacenter edition
- SQL Server 2008 R2 SP2 Standard, Datacenter edition
- SQL Server 2012 Enterprise, Standard (64-bit) edition
- SQL Server 2012 SP1 Enterprise, Standard (64-bit) edition

System Center 2012 R2 App Controller scaling limitations

System Center 2012 R2 App Controller has the following scaling and performance limitations:

Description	Value
Maximum number of SCVMM management servers	5
Maximum number of Windows Azure subscriptions per user	20
Maximum number of concurrent users	75
Maximum number of jobs that can be run in a 24-hour interval	10,000
Maximum number of objects in a Windows Azure storage directory	900

Summary

In this chapter, you learned the history of App Controller. Then we looked at the prerequisites required for successful installation. We also looked at the Microsoft supported versions of components. Finally, we looked at the limitations of App Controller.

In the next chapter, we will install prerequisites, required services, SQL Server, and App Controller.

2

Installing and Working with Different App Controller Components

In this chapter, we will start with the installation of SQL Server. Then we will move on to prepare the App Controller server for installation of System Center 2012 R2 App Controller. We will finish off with the installation of the App Controller service. After reading this chapter, you will be able to perform the following tasks:

- Installation of SQL Server 2012 Service Pack 1
- Installation of prerequisites for App Controller
- Installation of the IIS Server role
- Installation of System Center 2012 R2 App Controller

Installing SQL Server

System Center 2012 R2 App Controller requires an instance of SQL Server to store critical data. In this section, we will be preparing an instance of SQL 2012 Service Pack 1 for App Controller. At the time of writing this book, App Controller supports the following versions of SQL Server to host the App Controller database:

SQL Server edition	Service pack	Architecture
SQL Server 2008 R2 Datacenter	Service Pack 2	x86 and x64
SQL Server 2008 R2 Enterprise	Service Pack 2	x86 and x64
SQL Server 2008 R2 Standard	Service Pack 2	x86 and x64
SQL Server 2012 Standard	None	x86 and x64
SQL Server 2012 Enterprise	None	x86 and x64
SQL Server 2012 Standard	Service Pack 1	x86 and x64
SQL Server 2012 Enterprise	Service Pack 1	x86 and x64

We will be installing Microsoft SQL Server 2012 Service Pack 1. App Controller simply needs a supported instance to store data in the database. We require at least a database engine feature to host databases, but we will also be installing SQL management tools.

Attach the downloaded ISO file from the Microsoft licensing portal, or simply obtain a trial version from Microsoft. Attach or copy the media to the server that will be hosting the SQL Server services. In our case, it's `contoso-sql02.contoso.internal`:

1. Before we start the SQL Server installation wizard, create a domain user account in Active Directory users and computers. This account will be used as an SQL Service account later during installation. We also need to enable **.Net Framework 3.5 Features** by launching **Server Manager** and adding the features, as shown in the following screenshot:

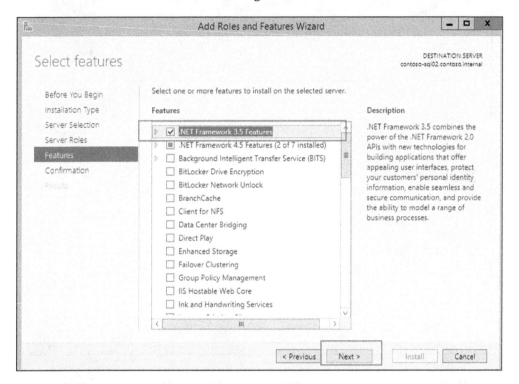

2. Select the **Restart the destination server automatically if required** option. Adding this feature will require the installation media attached to the server. Click on the **Specify an alternate source path** link at the bottom of the wizard, as shown in the following screenshot, and type `<drive letter>:\ sources\sxs\` in **Path**:

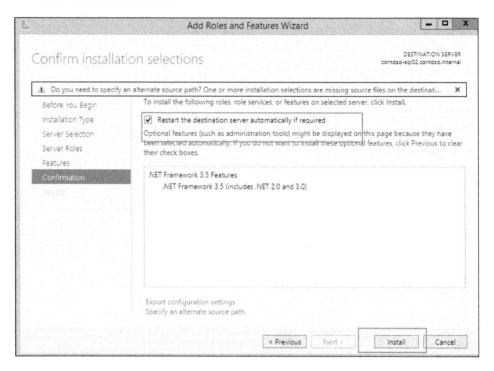

3. Then add the SQL Service account to the **Local Administrators** group on the designated SQL server.

4. Now browse to the location of the SQL Server installation media. Right-click on `Setup.exe` and select **Run as Administrator**.

5. Once **SQL Server Installation Center** launches, select **Installation** from the left pane and then select the **New SQL Server stand-alone installation or add features to an existing installation** link, as shown in this screenshot:

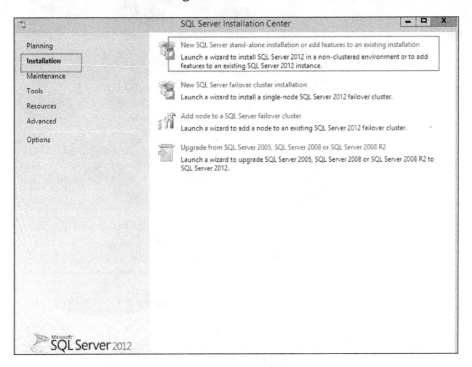

6. After **Setup Support Rules** have run successfully, click on the **OK** button.

7. Insert your **Registration key** details provided by Microsoft. We will be installing the trial version. Click on **Next**.

8. Accept **End User License Agreement**. Then click on **Next**.

9. After **Support Files** have been installed successfully, click on **Next**.

10. Leave the default selection and click on **Next**, as shown in the following screenshot:

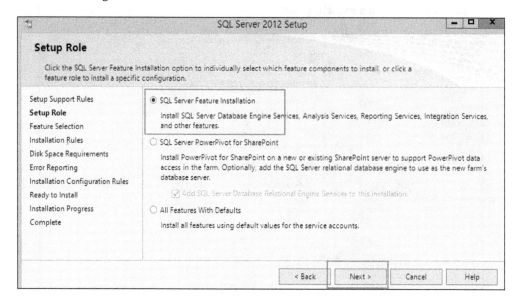

11. Select **Database Engine Services** and **Management Tools - Complete**, as shown in this screenshot:

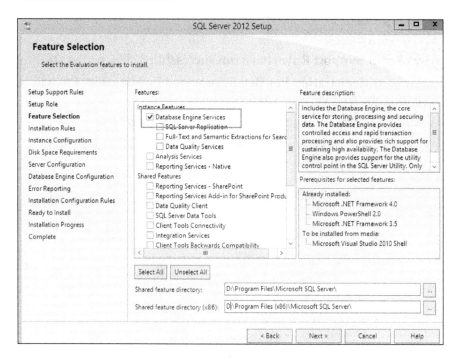

12. For better performance with databases, change the installation path to a non-system drive. I have already added a D drive to the SQL Server dedicated for the database files. After making all the changes, click on **Next** as shown in the following screenshot:

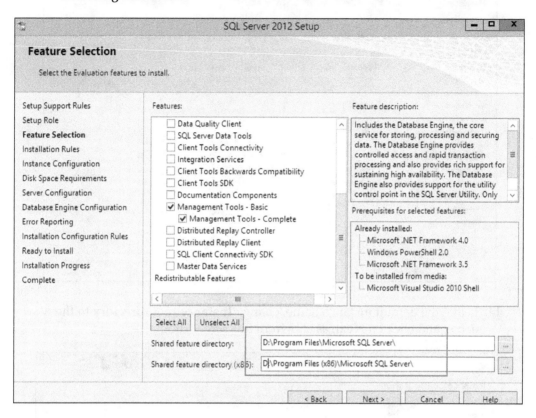

13. After the installation rules have been run successfully, click on **Next**, as shown in the following screenshot:

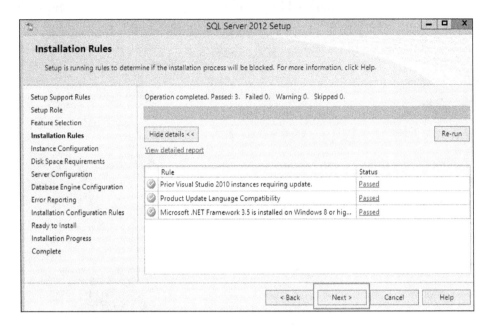

14. Leave the default instance name, change **Instance root directory** to the D drive, and click on **Next**, as shown in this screenshot:

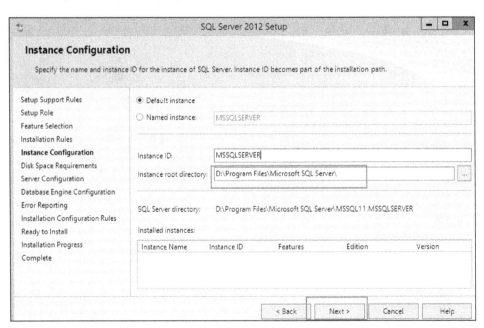

15. Review the disk requirements page as shown in the following screenshot, and then click on **Next**:

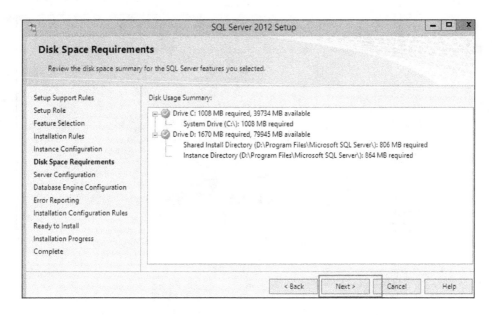

16. Change the SQL Service account to designated service accounts. In our case, it is a domain user account created for SQL services that is `srv_sql_acc`. We will be changing **SQL Server Database Engine** and the **SQL Server Agent** account. Then switch to the **Collation** tab, as shown in this screenshot:

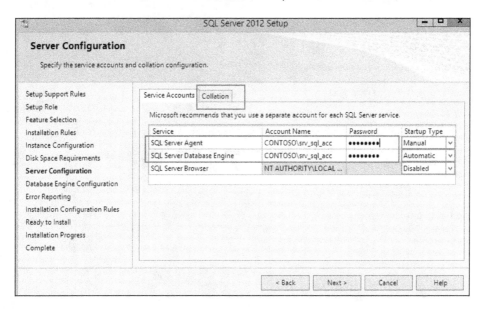

17. Click on **Customize** and select **SQL_Latin1_General_CP1_CI_AS** as the collation type, as shown in the following screenshot:

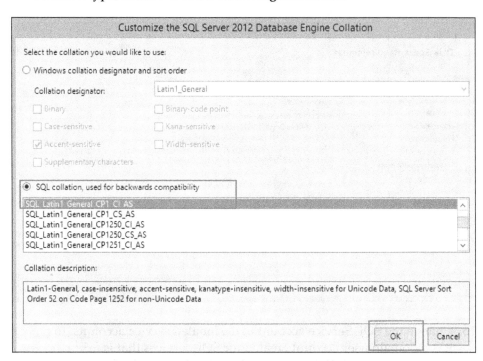

18. After changing **Collation**, click on **Next** as shown in this screenshot:

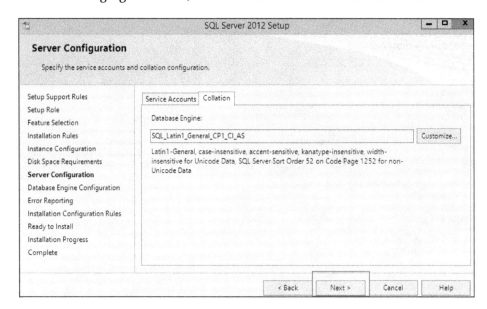

19. Leave **Authentication mode** as the default value of **Windows Authentication**. Add your own users or groups that require access to the SQL Server administration or troubleshooting here. Then click on **Next**.

20. Make a choice according to your enterprise to send error reports to Microsoft. We won't be sending error reports to Microsoft, so click on **Next**.

21. After **Installation Configuration Rules** has run successfully, click on **Next**, as shown in the following screenshot:

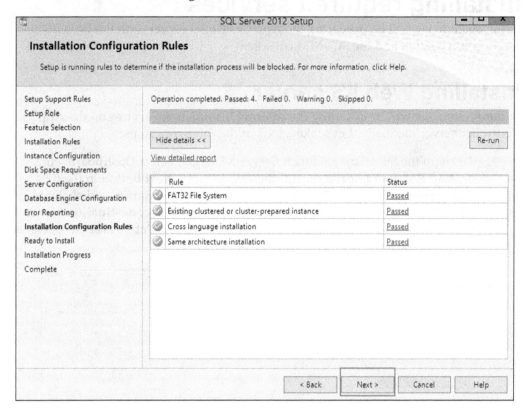

22. Review the information gathered during setup from the wizard. Note the location of the log files. Then click on **Install**. This is a good time for a coffee break. By default, the configuration file is created at `C:\Program Files\Microsoft SQL Server\110\Setup Bootstrap\Log\<Date of Installation>\ConfigurationFile.ini`.

23. After successful installation, review the installed features and then click on **Close**.

24. Log on to SQL Server using SQL Server Management Studio to confirm that the SQL services are running.

25. If the connection fails for any reason, then launch **SQL Server Configuration Manager Console** to check whether the **SQL Server (MSSQLSERVER)** instance is started.

26. An alternative method is to launch **Services console**. Check the status of the **SQL Server (MSSQLSERVER)** service.

Installing required services

In this section, we will be preparing the App Controller server with the Web IIS server configuration and the SCVMM console.

Installing Web IIS server

In this section, we will be installing the Internet Information Services on the App Controller server manually. Let's take a look at the following steps:

1. To begin the installation, launch **Server Manager**. Select **Dashboard**, click on **Add Roles and Features**, and then click on the **Next** button in the first dialog page. Select **Role-based or feature-based installation** and click on **Next**. Leave the default settings as they are in the **Select destination server** dialog box and click on **Next**. We will be adding the **Web Server (IIS)** role, as shown in the following screenshot:

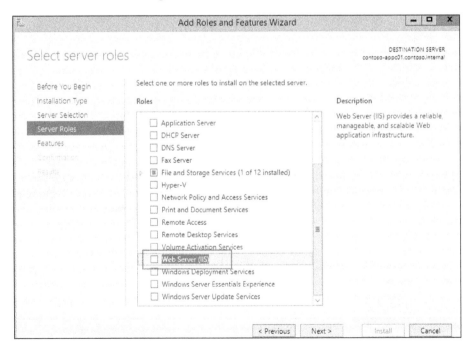

2. Select **Web Server (IIS)** and select **Add Features** in the dialog box that pops up. Then click on **Next**.

3. Click on the **Next** button in the features' dialog box, leaving the settings at default. In the **Web Server (IIS)** roles dialog box, the features that should be selected during the IIS installation are **Static Content, Default Document, Directory Browsing, HTTP Errors, ASP.NET, .NET Extensibility, ISAPI Extensions, ISAPI Filters, HTTP Logging, Request Monitor, Tracing, Basic Authentication, Windows Authentication, Request Filtering, Static Content Compression**, and **IIS Management Console**.

4. After selecting the required features, click on **Next**.

5. Review the list of selected features, and then click on **Install**.

Installing the SCVMM console

In this section, we will install the System Center Virtual Machine Manager console on the App Controller server. Extract and copy SCVMM 2012 R2 Media to the App Controller server. Then perform the following steps:

1. Browse to the folder where you copied the installation media. Right-click on the **Setup.exe** file and select **Run as administrator**.

2. Once the wizard launches, select the **Install** link, as shown in the following screenshot:

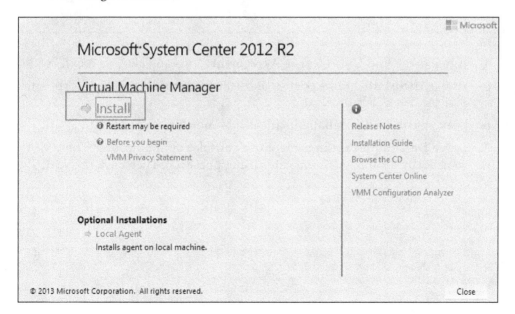

3. Click on the checkbox next to **VMM console**, and then click on Next, as shown in this screenshot:

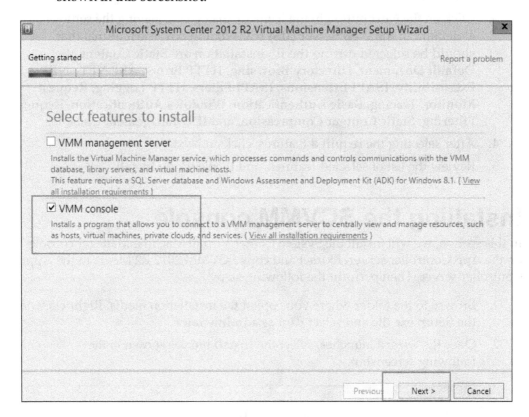

4. Agree to the **End User License Agreement** terms and click on **Next**.

5. At the **Microsoft Update** page, make a choice according to your corporate policies. Then click on **Next**.

6. Leave the default installation path as it is and click on **Next**.

7. Leave **Default port settings** for VMM console communication. The VMM console, by default, communicates using port **8100**. Then click on **Next**.

8. Review the settings and click on **Install**, as shown in the following screenshot:

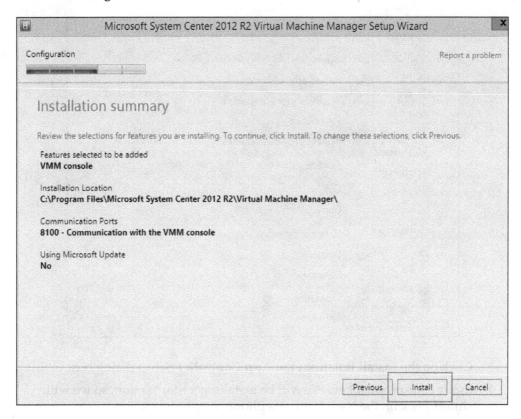

9. After the SCVMM console has been successfully installed, click on **Close**.

Installing System Center 2012 R2 App Controller

In this section, we will be installing System Center 2012 R2 App Controller on the `contoso-app01.contoso.internal` server. Copy or mount the installation media to the server.

1. I have created a domain user service account for App Controller, called `srv_scac_acc`. Add this account to the **Local Administrator** group on the App Controller server using the **Computer Management** snap-in console.

2. Extract the files by running the wizard. Right-click on **Setup.exe** and select **Run as administrator**, as shown in the following screenshot:

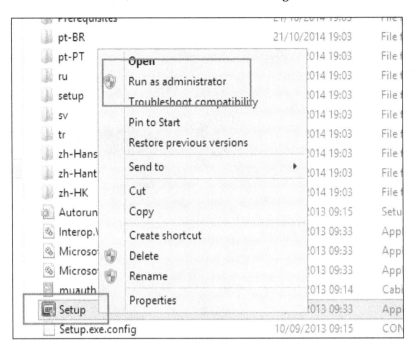

3. Click on the **Install** link from the **App Controller Setup** dialog box.

4. Input your product key. We will be installing a trial version, so we will simply click on the **Next** button, without any product key.

5. Accept the **End User License Agreement** and click on **Next**.

6. Click on the **Install** button to install the missing software page.

7. Leave the default settings at the installation path page and click on **Next**.

8. Provide the **Domain account** name details for the App Controller service, leave the default internal communication port of **18622** as it is, and click on **Next**, as shown in the following screenshot:

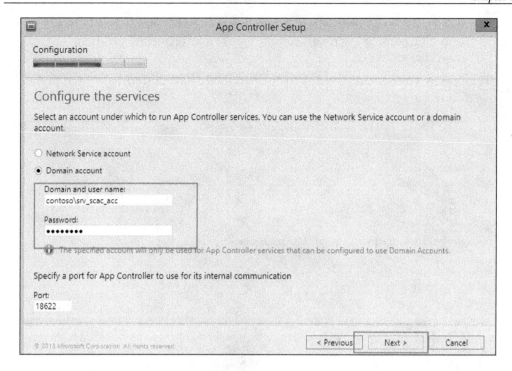

9. Select **Generate self-signed certificate** and click on **Next**.

10. Provide the details of SQL Server and then click on **Next**, as shown in this screenshot:

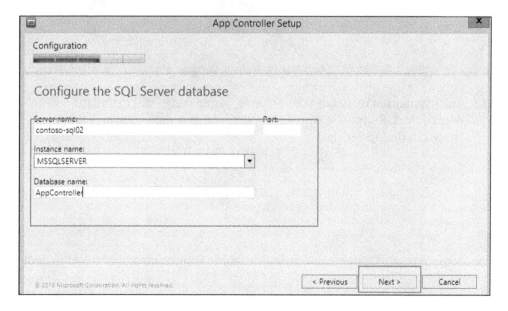

11. Make a choice according to your environment's requirements. I always send data back to Microsoft so that they can improve the product. Then click on **Next**.

12. Review your settings and then click on the **Install** button, as shown in the following screenshot:

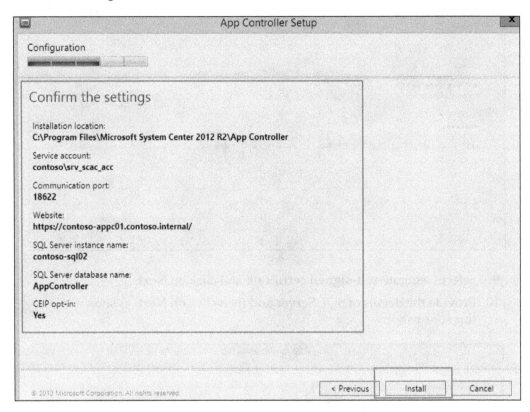

13. The installation does not take too long. After successful installation, take note of the URL for the App Controller site, and then click on **Finish**, as shown in this screenshot:

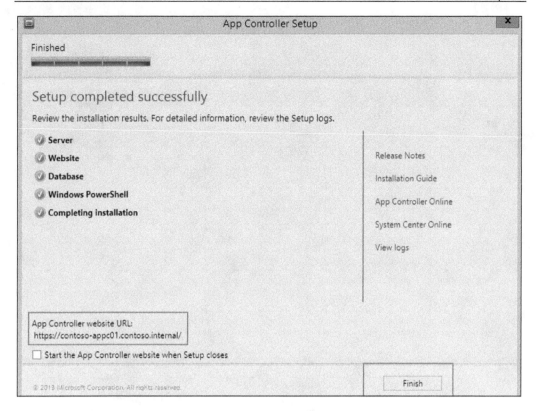

14. Ensure that the firewall ports are open to allow access to the App Controller server.

15. This concludes the installation of System Center 2012 R2 App Controller.

Summary

In this chapter, we installed the prerequisites of App Controller for a successful installation. This included setting up SQL Server and prestaging the required services. Then we installed System Center 2012 R2 App Controller.

In the next chapter, we will go through the steps to install and configure System Center 2012 R2 Virtual Machine Manager.

3
Deploying and Configuring System Center Virtual Machine Manager Server

System Center 2012 R2 App Controller enables the private cloud management feature by integrating with System Center Virtual Machine Manager. This chapter will provide step-by-step instructions for successful deployment of Virtual Machine Manager service. In this chapter, we will cover the following topics:

- Prerequisites of SCVMM installation
- Installation of the SCVMM service
- Configuration of SCVMM objects

One of the key requirements for successful Virtual Machine Manager installation is availability of supported SQL Server. SQL Server will be hosting the `Virtual Manager DB` database. This database contains SCVMM configuration and critical data for the service. For help with installation of SQL Server, review the *Installing SQL Server* section of *Chapter 2, Installing and Working with Different App Controller Components*.

Download installation media from the Microsoft website. Attach or copy extracted media to the server that will be hosting the SQL Server services.

Prerequisites for installation

In this section, we will be installing the necessary prerequisites before installation of Virtual Machine Manager.

Installing ADK 8.1

For instructions on the installation of ADK 8.1, refer to the *Windows assessment and deployment kit* for *Windows 8.1* section in *Chapter 1, Introduction to System Center 2012 R2 App Controller*.

Account permission requirements

The Virtual Machine Manager service requires elevated access to some server roles. The following are the settings that need to be configured before starting the installation of the VMM server:

- Create a standard domain user account in Active Directory's users and computers. Then add it to the local administrators security group on the VMM server. We created an srv_vmm account. A restart is recommended after adding the account to the local administrators group.

- Add the VMM server computer account to the local administrator group on a designated SQL server. A restart is recommended after adding the computer account to the local administrators group.

Installing System Center 2012 R2 Virtual Machine Manager

In this section, we will be installing System Center 2012 R2 Virtual Machine Manager. Copy or mount the installation media onto the server by performing the following steps:

1. We have created a service account for VMM Service, named srv_vmm. Add this account to the local administrators group on the VMM server.

2. Extract the files by running the wizard. Right-click on the Setup.exe folder and select **Run as administrator**.

3. Click on the **Install** link, as shown in the following screenshot:

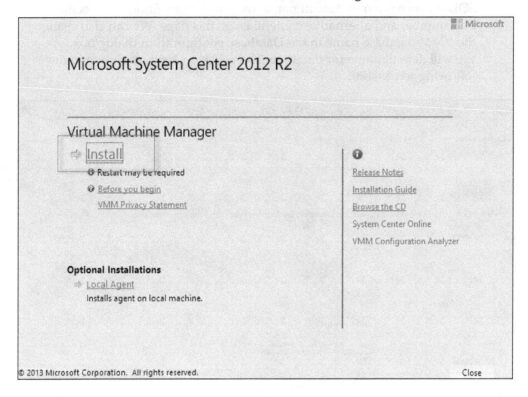

4. Select **VMM management server** on the **Select features to install** dialog box. Then click on **Next**.

5. On the **Product registration information** dialog box page, provide **Name**, **Organization** and **Product key**. Then click on **Next**.

6. Read and select the checkbox next to **I have read, understood, and agree with the terms of the license agreement**. Then click on **Next**.

7. Select an appropriate choice according to your organization in the **Customer Experience Improvement Program** dialog box. Then click on **Next**.

8. Select **Off** in the **Microsoft Update** dialog box. Then click on **Next**.

9. Leave the default path for installation of the VMM server as it is on the **Installation location** page. The default path is `C:\Program Files\ Microsoft System Center 2012 R2\Virtual Machine Manager`. Then click on **Next**.

10. Resolve any issues that show up on the **Warnings** page, which is a prerequisite. Then click on **Next**.

11. On the **Database configuration** page, provide the SQL **Server name**. If the
    SQL instance is a non-default name, we can even mention the specific
    port number and alternative credentials on this page. We can also change
    the VMM database name in the **Database configuration** dialog box.
    We will default name for database. Then click on **Next**, as shown in the
    following screenshot:

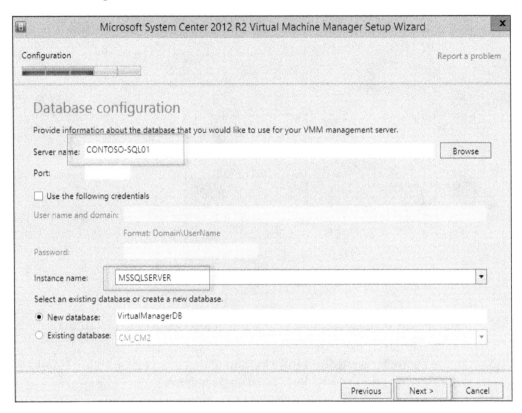

12. On the **Configure service account and distributed key management**
    page, provide the **Domain account** name that we have created earlier.
    This page also allows us to configure the **Distributed Key Management**
    settings to store the management keys in the Active Directory. Storing
    management keys in the Active Directory is a safer automated method
    than storing it locally on the VMM server. In a highly available VMM
    configuration, a distributed key has to be stored in the Active Directory.
    More details about these keys can be found at `http://go.microsoft.com/`
    `fwlink/?linkid=209609`. After providing the **Domain account** credentials,
    click on **Next**.

13. On the **Port configuration** page, review and take note of the communication ports that will be used by the VMM server. Then click on **Next**, as shown in the following screenshot:

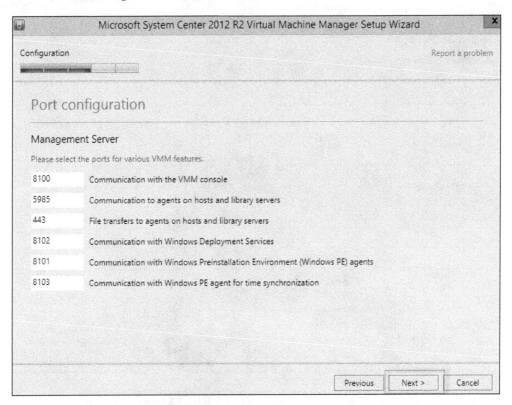

14. On the **Library configuration** page, leave the default location as it is and click on **Next**.

15. Review the selected features and then click on **Install**.

16. After the installation is successfully finished, click on the **Close** button, as shown in this screenshot:

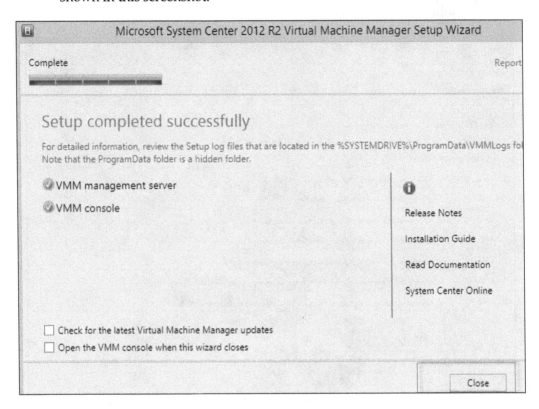

This concludes the installation of System Center Virtual Machine Manager.

Configuring the SCVMM server

Log on to the VMM server. Launch the VMM console by double-clicking on the **Virtual Machine Manager Console** icon on the desktop, as shown here:

VMM console is divided into five different sections: **VMs and Services**, **Fabric**, **Library**, **Jobs**, and **Settings**. All of these sections can be seen in the left pane, as shown in the following screenshot:

The **VMs and Services** section can show configured Tenants, Clouds, VM Networks, Storage, and All Hosts components.

The **Fabric** section is further subdivided into Servers, Networking, and Storage. The **Servers** subsection contains infrastructure building components such as Library Servers, PXE servers, Update Server, vCenter Servers, and VMM Server.

The **Networking** section contains Logical Networks, MAC Address Pools, Load Balancers, VIP Templates, Logical Switches, Port Profiles, Port Classifications, and Network Service.

The **Storage** section contains Classifications and Pools, Providers, Arrays, File Servers, and Fibre Channel Fabric resources.

The **Library** section contains Templates, Service Templates, VM Templates, Service Deployment Configuration, Profiles, Hardware Profiles, Operating System Profiles, Cloud Libraries, Library Servers, Self Service User Content, and Update Catalog and Baselines.

We need at least one cloud configured in Virtual Machine Manager so that App Controller can display the configuration and templates assigned to the resources.

Adding Hyper-V host to the SCVMM server

To add a Hyper-V host to the VMM server, perform the following steps:

1. Launch **VMM Console**. Click on **Fabric** in the left pane. Click on **Servers**, then click on **Add Resources** in the top ribbon, and select **Hyper-V Hosts and Clusters**, as shown in the following screenshot. This will launch **Add Hyper-V Host** wizard.

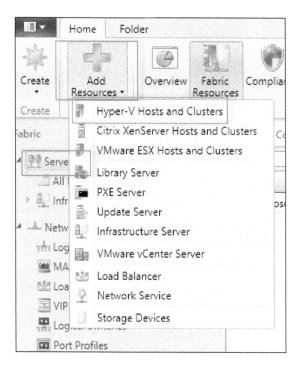

2. Select **Windows Sever** computers in a trusted Active Directory domain. Then click on **Next**.

3. At the **Specify the credentials to use for discovery** page, specify **Run as account** that has local administrator access to the Hyper-V host. Then click on **Next**.

4. On **Specify the search scope for virtual machine host candidates**, select **Specify Windows Server computers by names**. After specifying the Hyper-V hostname, click on **Next**.

5. Select the discovered computer from the list in the **Target Resources** pages. Then click on **Next**.

6. On the **Specify a host group and virtual machine placement path settings for hosts** page, add the Hyper-V host to the default option or a specific **Host Group**. Then click on **Next**.

7. Confirm the settings on the **Summary** page. We can also save the PowerShell script for the purpose of automation. Then click on **Finish**.

8. Wait for the VMM job to finish adding the Hyper-V host.

This concludes adding the Hyper-V host to the VMM server.

Creating hardware profiles

The following steps will walk you through the tasks required to create a new hardware profile:

1. Launch **VMM Console** and select the **Library** button in the left pane. Expand **Profiles**, right-click on **Hardware Profiles**, and select **Create Hardware Profile** from the pop-up menu.

2. After the **New Hardware Profile** wizard launches, provide a unique name for the profile. It's good practice to name the profile according to the services being offered. We will be using `Small HW Size Windows Server 2012 R2`.

3. Provide a good description and select the generation for **Hardware Profile**. We will be using the default, which is **Generation 1**.

4. Switch to the **Hardware Profiles** tab in the left pane. In the **Cloud Capability** section, select the checkbox next to **Hyper-V**. In the **Processor** section, select **Appropriate number of processors**. In the **Memory** section, we will be using **Static Memory** of **2048 MB**. In the **Networking** section, select a **VM network**. Finally, in the **Availability** section, select the checkbox next to **Make this virtual machine highly available** if the virtual machine will be residing on a Hyper-V cluster. In our case, it's a standalone Hyper-V machine, so we won't be selecting this option.

5. There are many more settings that can be configured for **Hardware Profiles** in this section, but they are out of the scope of this book. Once the preceding settings are configured, click on **OK** as shown in the following screenshot:

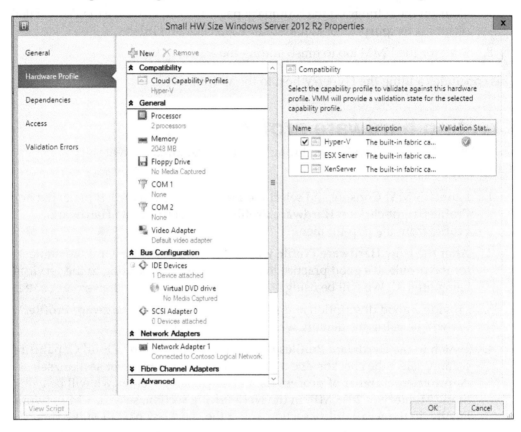

6. We can have multiple **Hardware Profiles** to address the needs of the corporate end user, while also enforcing corporate policies and standardizing virtual machine configurations. The end user does not need to know where these resources are going to be created and information related to the backend of the infrastructure. These will be configured by the VMM administrator. Take a look at the following screenshot:

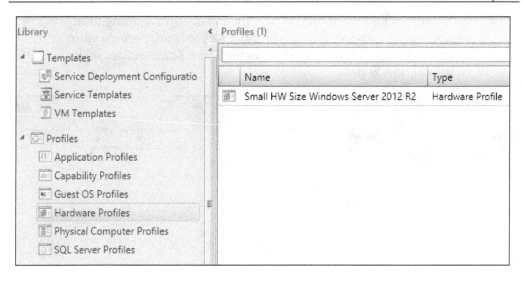

Creating Guest OS profiles

Guest operating system profiles allow the VMM server to apply a computer name pattern, compatibility, product key, local administrator credentials, time zone, domain join credentials, and answer files to a single package. We can also add roles and features during virtual machine deployment. The following steps will walk you through the procedure of creating a Guest OS profile:

1. Launch **VMM Console**, select **Library** from the left pane, and expand **Profiles**.

2. Right-click on **Guest OS Profiles** and select **Create Guest OS Profile** from the pop-up menu.

   Once the **Create New Guest OS profile** wizard launches, provide a unique name. We will be using OS Profile Windows Server 2012 R2, and will provide a good description for the OS profile. Leave **Compatibility** to the default setting of **Microsoft Windows**.

3. Switch to the **Guest OS Profile** tab in the left pane. In the **General settings** section, select **Operating System** and **Windows Server 2012 R2 Standard**. In the **Identity information** section, replace the asterisk with Contoso-Web_###. This will allow VMM to assign a sequence number during the provisioning process. If we leave the asterisk in **Computer name** as it is, a random name will be generated each time a new virtual machine is deployed.

4. In the **Admin password** section, specify and confirm a strong local administrative password. In the **Product Key** section, provide your corporate **VLK** or **MAK** key. Then, in the **Time Zone** section, select your local time zone.

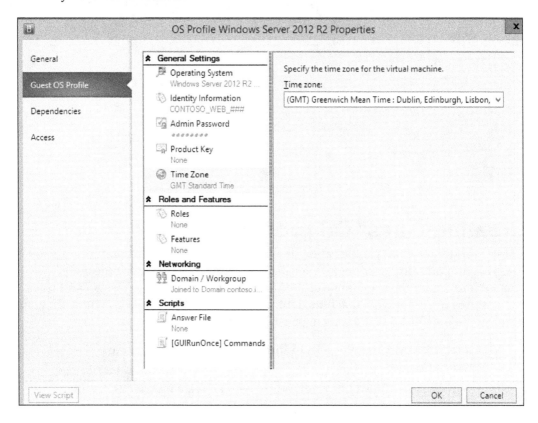

5. In the **Networking** section, specify **Domain name** and **User account credentials** details that have enough permission to join a machine to the domain.

6. When all the details have been provided, click on **OK**.

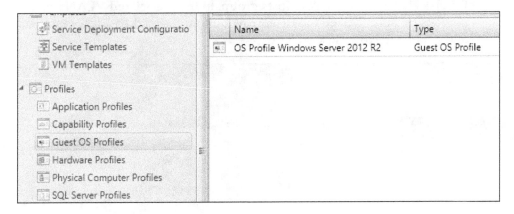

Creating a VM network

In this section, we will be creating a VM network that will be assigned to a private cloud later. Perform the following instructions to create a new VM network:

1. Launch **VMM Console** and select **Fabric** in the left pane.

2. Expand **Networking**, right-click on **Logical Networks**, and select **Create Logical Network** from the pop-up menu.

3. In the **Name** field, provide a unique name. We will be using `Contoso Logical Network`. Under the **One connected network** section, select the checkbox next to **Allow new VM networks created on this logical network to use network virtualization**, and also check the box next to **Create a VM network with the same name to allow virtual machines to access this logical network directly**. Then click on **Next**.

4. In the **Network Site** tab, click on the **Add** button. On the right side, select the checkbox next to the **All Hosts** group. In the **Associated VLANs and IP subnets** section, click on the **Insert row** button. Then add a VLAN number and IP subnet. Now click on **Next**.

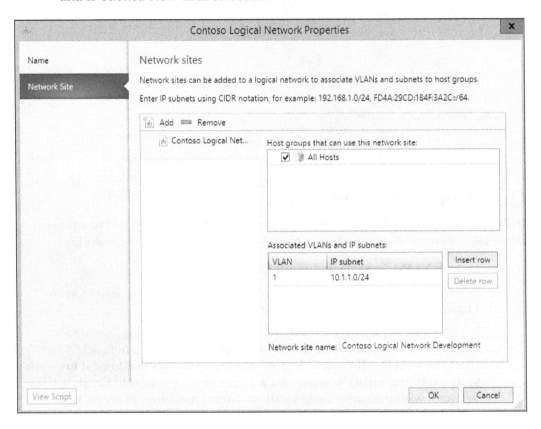

5. Review **Settings** and click on the **Finish** button.

6. In a single wizard, we were able to configure a logical network and a virtual network. We also have the ability to add multiple subnets and VLANs to a single logical network. Such settings are out of the scope of this book.

7. Right-click on **Contoso Logical Network** and select **Create IP Pool**. Here, we create an IP pool, and it is assigned to a particular logical network for automatic distribution of IPs. Newly provisioned virtual machines will receive IPs from this pool of addresses.

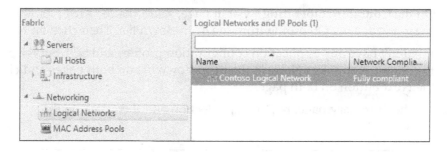

8. Step through **Create IP Pool wizard** to define the IP address distribution to VMs. Provide a unique name for **IP Pool**, **Logical network**, and **Description**. Then click on **Next**.

9. We will use an existing network site that was created earlier, and then click on **Next**.

10. Specify the starting and ending ranges and click on **Next**.

11. Specify the **Gateway**, **DNS**, and **WINS** settings according to your environment. Then click on **Next**.

12. On the **Summary** page, review the settings and click on **Finish**.

Creating the VM template

Now that we have all the building blocks configured in the VMM server, we will create a VM template. Perform the following steps to configure a new VM template:

1. Launch **VMM Console**. Select **Library** in the left pane.

2. Expand **Templates**, right-click on **VM Templates**, and select **Create VM Template** from the pop-up menu.

3. Click on the **Browse** button in **Use an existing VM template or a virtual hard disk stored in the library**.

4. Select a VHD or VHDx file that has been prepared for storage in the VMM library. I have a Windows Server 2012 R2 file already imported. Click on **OK** after selecting the appropriate file.

5. Now you will be taken back to the **Create VM Template** wizard. Click on **Next**.

6. Provide a unique name in **VM Template Name**. We will be using Windows Server 2012 R2 WEB Template. Provide a good description, leave **Generation type** to the default value of **Generation 1**, and click on **Next**.

7. On the **Configure Hardware** page, select the Small HW Size Windows Server 2012 R2 hardware profile from the drop-down list. Then click on **Next**.

8. On the **Configure Operating System** page, select the `OS Profile Windows Server 2012 R2` OS profile from the drop-down list. Then click on **Next**.

9. We don't have any application configuration profiles and SQL Server profiles to configure, so select **None** in the drop-down list on both pages and click on the **Next** button on both pages.

10. On the **Summary** page, review the selection and then click on the **Create** button.

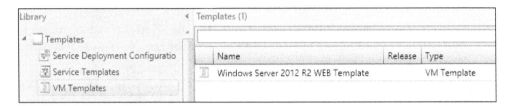

Creating a private cloud

In this section, we will be combining all the pieces of the puzzle into a single entity called cloud. We have the ability to create multi-tenant environment on a single physical hardware or cluster. Perform the following steps to configure a cloud in the VMM server environment:

1. Launch **VMM Console** if it is not already open. Select **VMs and Services** from the left pane.

2. Right-click on **Clouds** and select **Create Cloud** from the pop-up menu.

3. On the **General** page, specify a unique name and description for the cloud. We will be using `Contoso Cloud` as the name. Then click on **Next**.

4. On the **Resource** page, select the appropriate **Host Group** (we will be using **All Hosts** group) and then click on **Next**.

5. On the **Logical Network** page, select an appropriate logical network. Then click on **Next**.

6. Click on **Next** on the **Load Balancers** and **VIP Templates** pages.

7. On the **Port Classifications** page, select the appropriate port classifications that should be allowed for this cloud, and then click on **Next**.

8. On the **Storage** page, select the appropriate storage classifications according to your environment. Then click on **Next**.

9. On the **Library** page, click on the **Add** button, select the default **VMM Library**, and click on **OK**. Then click on **Next**.

10. On the **Capacity** page, leave default settings of **Unlimited capacity** as they are, and click on **Next**.

11. On the **Capability Profiles** page, select **Hyper-V**. Then click on **Next**.

12. On the **Summary** page, review the selections and click on **Finish**.

Summary

In this chapter, we installed the prerequisites for successful installation of System Center 2012 R2 Virtual Machine Manager. Then we configured hardware profiles, guest OS profiles for automation of Virtual Machine deployment. We also created a VM template to consolidate hardware and guest OS profiles. Then we created a logical network and VM network to route data from virtual machines.

In the next chapter, we will continue with System Center 2012 R2 App Controller, integrate the VMM server with App Controller and Azure Subscription, and add a network share.

Customizing App Controller

4

System Center 2012 R2 App Controller provides a web-based portal to manage an on-premises Azure Cloud and a third party cloud solution through a single pane of glass. Before we can manage these solutions, we will need to connect to these resources by integrating them in the App Controller admin console. This chapter will walk you through the steps required for integration.

In this chapter, we will cover the following topics:

- Getting familiar with the App Controller admin console
- Connecting Virtual Machine Manager with App Controller
- Connecting to Azure subscription
- Adding network shared storage to App Controller
- Changing the SSL certificate on the App Controller admin portal website

In previous chapters, we installed App Controller. For help with App Controller installation, refer to *Chapter 2, Installing and Working with Different App Controller Components*.

Logging in to the App Controller interface

In this section, we will log in to the App Controller web portal for the first time. Perform the following steps to open the App Controller admin console:

1. Before attempting to log on to the App Controller server, ensure that Microsoft Silverlight is installed on the server. It can be downloaded from `http://www.microsoft.com/silverlight/`.

2. Log on to the App Controller server. Launch the Internet Explorer: type `https://localhost`, and press the *Enter* key.

3. If a warning message saying **There is a problem with this website's security certificate** shows up, select the **Continue to this website (not recommended)** link, as shown in the following screenshot:

4. Now, you will be presented with the logon screen. Provide administrative credentials to log on to start with, it is the service account details of the App Controller administrator. Click on the **Sign In** button in the browser as follows:

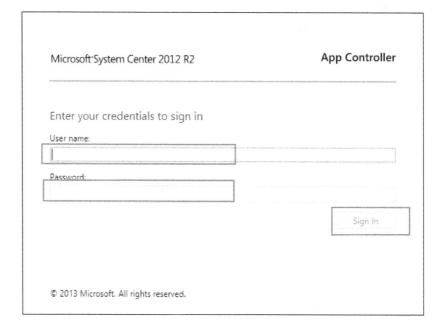

5. Depending on the speed of your system, the Microsoft System Center 2012 R2 App Controller Admin portal will open. The Admin portal is based on the Silverlight technology and looks very similar to the Virtual Machine Manager Console as follows:

6. The App Controller Admin console is divided into seven sections, as shown in the left pane of the preceding screenshot. By default, the **Overview** page shows up every time we log in to the admin portal. We can manage multiple subscriptions and common tasks in the **Overview** page. There are three main categories in the **Overview** page. Out of them, **Status** contains **Private Clouds** created in the VMM server, **Public Clouds** displays Microsoft Azure subscriptions being managed by App Controller, and **Hosting Service Providers** shows third party service providers.

Integrating the Virtual Machine Manager server for private cloud management

In this section, we will integrate our previously installed Virtual Machine Manager server with the App Controller server. Perform the following steps to complete the task:

1. Log on to the App Controller server. Launch Internet Explorer and log in with an account that has local administrative access on the App Controller server. On the **Overview** page, under the **Private Clouds** subsection of the **Status** section, click on the **Connect a Virtual Machine Manager server** link, as shown in the following screenshot. In future, we should click on the **Settings** link in the left pane, select **Connections** in the submenu, click on **Connect** in the middle pane, and select **SCVMM** from the pop-up menu.

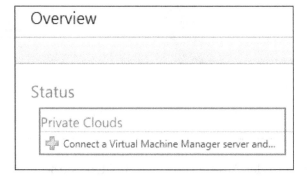

2. In the pop-up dialog box, provide a **Connection Name**, **Description**, **Server name**, and a **Port** for VMM communication. Ensure that you select **Automatically import SSL certificates**. Then click on the **OK** button as shown:

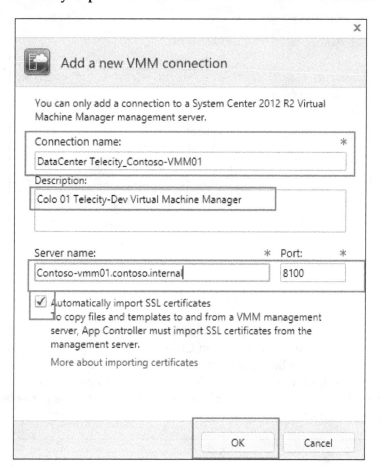

3. After a couple of minutes, VMM integration will be completed and the **Private Clouds** section will be populated with the current configuration set in the VMM server, as shown in the following screenshot:

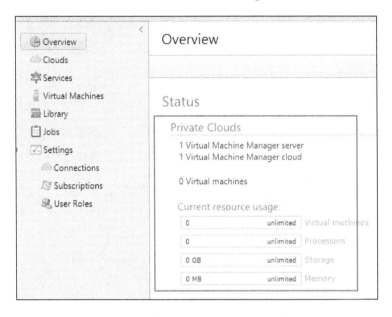

4. We can also see the configuration of the configured clouds in Virtual Machine Manager. By clicking on **Clouds** in the left pane, **Contoso Cloud** can be seen in the middle pane with a description and cloud name assigned. To see computer limitations set on the cloud, we can change the **View** option to show information cards by clicking on the **Show items as cards** button in the top-right corner:

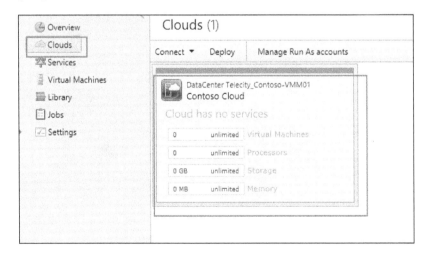

Configuring a Microsoft Azure subscription

In this section, we will configure the on-premises App Controller deployment to connect to the Windows Azure subscription. The following capabilities will be enabled for our private cloud users in both private and public cloud:

- Start virtual machines
- Stop virtual machines
- Shut down virtual machines
- Restart virtual machines
- Connect to virtual machines
- Modify existing virtual machines
- Copy existing virtual machines to Azure
- Deploy virtual machines
- Deploy cloud services
- Add virtual machines to cloud services
- Modify existing services
- View and manage jobs

To connect App Controller to Windows Azure, we have to first create a self-signed certificate. Then export the certificate package with private keys and also export the certificate without private keys. Next, we need to upload the certificate without private keys to the Windows Azure management portal and import the certificate package with the subscription ID into App Controller. Perform the following steps to complete the task:

1. Log on to the App Controller server and launch the IIS manager console.

2. Left-click on the **Server name** in the console. Double-click on **Server Certificates** in the **IIS** feature section, as follows:

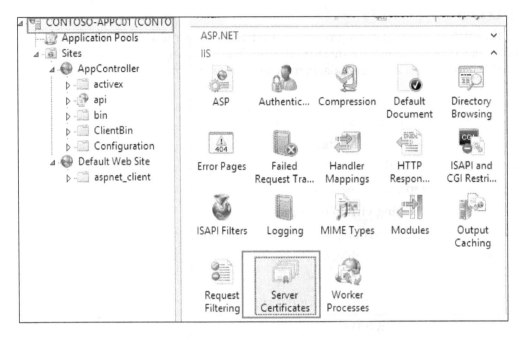

3. In the **Actions** pane on the right side of the console. Click on the **Create Self-Signed Certificate** link.

4. In the **Create Self-Signed Certificate** wizard, provide a friendly name like AzureManagementCertificate and store it in the **Personal** store. Then click on **OK**.

5. Launch **MMC** by typing MMC in the **Run** dialog box. Add **Certificate snap-in** from **Add/remove snap-ins**. Select **Computer account** for managing certificates store. Then click on **Next**.

6. In the **Select the computer you want this snap-in to manage** section dialog page, select **Local computer**. Next, click on **Finish** and then click on **OK**.

7. Back in the **MMC** console, expand **Certificates (Local Computer)**. Expand **Personal**, then **Highlight Certificates**. In the middle pane, we can see the list of certificates available.

8. Right-click on `AzureManagementCertificate`. Select **All Tasks** and click on **Export...**.

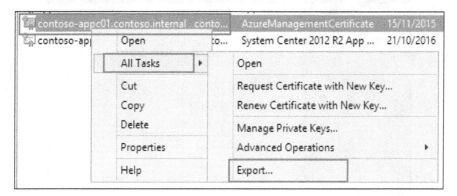

9. Click on **Next** to start the **Certificate Wizard**. Make sure the **Yes export the private key** option is selected. Then click on **Next**.

10. Leave default settings for **Export File Format** and click on **Next**. Provide a strong password to protect the PFX package. Then click on **Next**. Provide a path to store the package locally and click on **Next**. Finally, click on **Finish**.

11. Now log on to the **Windows Azure** portal. Sign in with your **Azure Administrative ID** details.

12. In the **Management Portal**, select **Settings** in the left pane. In the middle pane, click on the **MANAGEMENT CERTIFICATES** link. Then click on the **UPLOAD A MANAGEMENT CERTIFICATE** link as shown in the following screenshot. Browse for the **CER** file without private keys. Wait for the upload to complete. Take a note of the **Subscription ID** in the **Management Certificates** section. This will be used during the App Controller connection configuration.

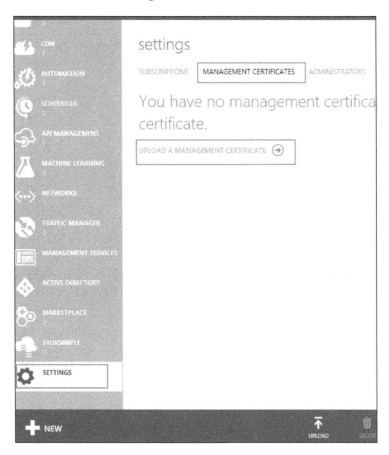

13. Now, we are ready to connect App Controller to the Azure subscription. Azure cloud subscription will use certificate authentication. The certificate uploaded in the previous step will be used for encrypting traffic between App Controller and Azure cloud.

14. Back in the **App Controller** admin portal, click on **Clouds** in the left pane. Click on the down arrow on the **Connect** button in the middle pane. Then select **Windows Azure subscription**, as shown in the following screenshot:

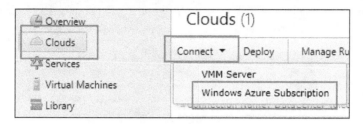

15. Provide a friendly name for the subscription and values for the **Description**, **Subscription ID**, and **Management certificate** fields with a private key and **Management certificate password** for the PFX package file. Then click on **OK**, as shown in the following screenshot:

16. After a couple of minutes, **Azure subscription** will be added to the App Controller environment. Now we can manage **Services** and **Virtual Machines** attached to this subscription, as follows:

17. In the **Cloud** section, we can also see the new **Windows Azure** connection as shown in the following screenshot:

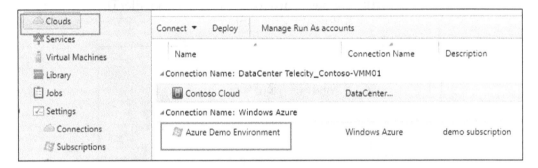

Configuring roles-based access

In this section, we will be adding a new tenant user to the App Controller. This user will be assigned particular settings to manage their environment. I have created a standard domain user called `Contoso_Tenant01` for demo purposes. This account will be given full administrative access to the **Contoso Cloud** only. Follow the following steps to complete this task:

1. Log on to the Virtual Machine Manager server. Launch **VMM Console**.

2. Select **Settings** in the left pane. Expand **Security** and select **User Roles**. In the ribbon, click on **Create User Role**, as shown in the following screenshot:

3. After the **Create User Role** wizard launches, provide the **Name** and **Description** and then click on **Next**. I have used **Contoso Cloud Administrator** and **Administrator of Contoso Cloud**.

4. Select **Tenant Administrator** and click on **Next**:

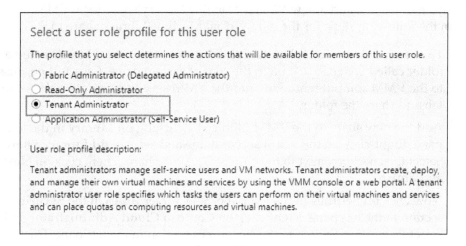

5. In the **Members** section, add a security group on individual user accounts. I have added a `Contoso_Tenant01` account to the members list. Then click on **Next**.

6. In the **Scope** section of the wizard, select the checkbox next to **Contoso Cloud** and click on **Next**.

7. In the **Quotas for the Contoso Cloud** section, adjust **Role Level** and **Member level quotas** as required. We will be using the default settings of **Use Maximum** for all settings. Then click on **Next**.

8. In the **Networking** section of the wizard, add **Logical network belonging to Contoso** by clicking on the **Add** button. Then click on **Next**.

9. In the **Resources** section of the wizard, add resources that this tenant administrator can use. I have selected **OS profiles**, **Small HW hardware profile**, **VM Template**, and **Service Template**, available in the list. Then click on **Next**.

10. In the **Permissions** section of the wizard, we can specify tasks that this user account can perform in the environment. Switch to **Contoso Cloud** in the middle pane. Click on the **Select All** button. Then click on **Next**

11. In the **Run As Accounts** section of the create **User Roles** wizard, specify a **privileged account** that is required in Contoso Cloud and click on **Next**.

12. In the **Summary** section of the wizard, review specified settings and then click on **Finish**.

Adding a new VMM Library share

In this section, we will add a new Virtual Machine Library share to SCVMM. Perform the following steps for the new Virtual Machine Library share to SCVMM:

1. To specify a dedicated folder to upload data by this user, I have created a folder called Contoso_Cloud in the root of system drive. Give full permission to the VMM computer account and the VMM service account on the security tab and share the folder.

2. Add the new share to the VMM Library by clicking on **Library** in the left pane. Right-click on the VMM server name.and select **Add Library Shares**. Select the checkbox next to the Contoso_Cloud share. Then, click on **Next** and **Finish**.

3. Now click on **Settings** in the left pane. Select **User Roles** in the **Security** section in the left pane. Right-click on **Contoso Cloud Administrator** and select **Properties**. Switch to the **Resources** section in the left pane. Click on the **Browse** button in the **Specify the library location where this user can upload data** section. Select the Contoso_Cloud folder from the **Select destination folder** dialog box and click on **OK**.

4. Now log on to the **App Controller** server. Open a new session in Internet Explorer and browse to the **App Controller** admin portal. Log on with a new account. In our case, it is `domainname\contoso_tenant01`, as shown in the following screenshot:

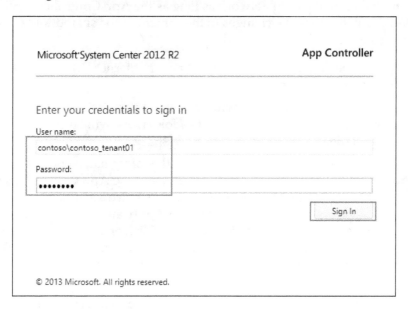

5. After logging on, the `Contoso_Tenant01` account can only see items that are allowed in the Virtual Machine Manager server, as follows:

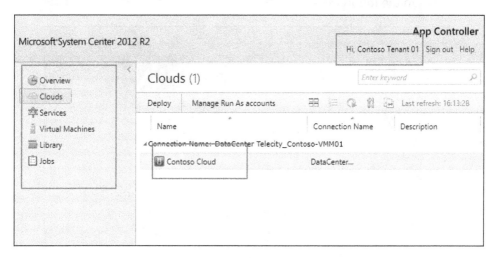

Adding a network share

In this section, we will be adding a network share to the App Controller server. This share will be used as local cache during download or upload of the virtual machines. It can be any folder on the local network as long as the App Controller service account has the ability to make changes to the content of the shared folder. Perform the following steps to complete this task:

1. Log on to the App Controller server. Launch Internet Explorer and log in with administrative credentials.

2. We also need a shared folder with the correct permissions assigned. So launch Windows Explorer and create a folder. We will be creating a folder in the root of the system drive called SCAC_Share.

3. Once the folder is created, right-click on the folder name and select **Properties**. Switch to the **Security** tab and add the **App Controller** service account. Give full control permission to the service account. In our case, the account name is srv_scac_acc. Click on **Apply** and then on **OK**. Repeat the same process by switching to **Sharing** tab. Click on the **Share** button. Add the service account if it is not already present and then click on the **Share** button. Now click on the **Done** button and click on the **Close** button on the folder properties dialog box.

4. Now go back to the Internet Explorer browser and select the **Overview** page in the App Controller admin portal. Under the **Next Steps** section in the **Common Tasks** subsection, click on the **Add a network file share** link, as shown in the following screenshot:

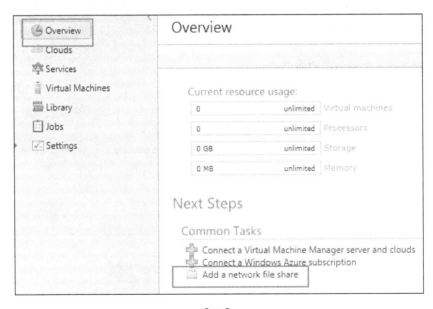

5. Provide the **UNC path** to the folder that we created in step 3. The naming syntax is \\<servername>\<sharename>. Then click on **OK**. A confirmation message will show up at the bottom of the screen for the task being completed. Take a look at the following screenshot:

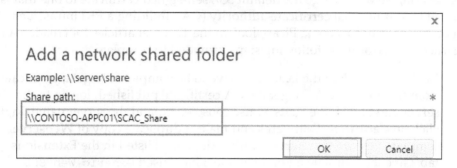

6. We can verify the addition of the share by clicking on **Library** in the left pane. Expanding **Shares** in the middle pane, we can also add more shares or remove listed shares in the Library's **Shares** section, as follows:

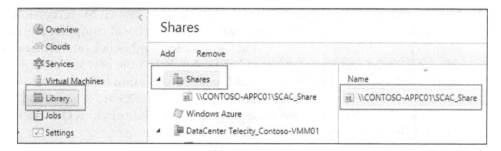

Configuring SSL certificate for the App Controller website

In this section, we will change the default SSL self-signed certificate to one that is generated by our internal **certificate authority (CA)**. Building a PKI infrastructure is out of the scope of this book. Please look at the TechNet articles for creating a PKI infrastructure. Perform the following steps provided to complete this task:

1. I will try to explain the tasks that have to be completed to get a certificate from the internal CA. To get the CA certificate published, log on to the CA server and launch the **Certsrv.msc** console. Expand the server name. Right-click on **Certificate Templates** and make a duplicate copy of **Webserver template**. Ensure that **Server Authentication** is listed in the **Extensions** tab. Give the template a unique name. I have used Generic Web SSL Certificate. In the **Security** tab, allow the **App Controller** server with the **Enroll** permission. Then right-click on **Certificates Templates** in the **Certsrv** console. Select **New**; select **New Certificate templates to issue**. From the list, select the new template.

2. Now, reboot the App Controller server. After reboot, launch **MMC console**, add certificates snap-in, and ensure that it shows the **Local computer** store. Then expand to **Personal** and expand **Certificates**. Right-click on **Certificates**, select **All Tasks** and **Request New Certificates**. Select the new template we just published and click on the **Add more information** link. Change **Type** from **FullDN** to **Common Name**. Specify appcontroller.contoso. internal. Give this certificate a friendly name and then click on **OK**. Back in the **Certificate enrolment wizard**, click on **Enroll**.

3. Log on to the App Controller server and launch the Internet Information Services console. The IIS Manager console can also be launched by pressing the windows key and typing in InetMgr.exe.

4. Expand **Server Name** and also expand **Sites**. Right-click on the **AppController** website. Select **Edit Bindings…**, as shown in the following screenshot:

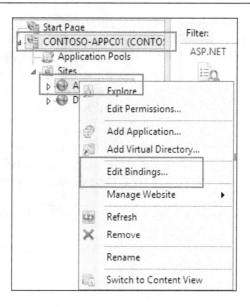

5. In the **Edit Sites Bindings** dialog box, select **https** and then click on the **Edit** button.

6. Select **appcontroller Webserver Cert** from the drop-down list. Verify that certificate is correct by clicking on the **View** button. Click on the **Select** button and then click on the **OK** button, as shown in the following screenshot:

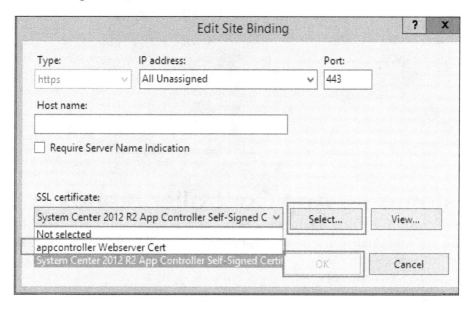

7. Now that we have a valid certificate assigned to the website in IIS Manager, create **Host (A) record** in DNS services. Specify `appcontroller.contoso.internal` as the **FQDN** and **IP address** of the App Controller server. Make sure **Silverlight** is installed on the testing machine. Launch Internet Explorer and browse to `https://appcontroller.contoso.internal`. After a couple of seconds, the App Controller logon screen will show up.

8. Take a look in the browser address bar; the certificate error should have disappeared. We no longer get a warning message before the log on screen. We can also verify the certificate assigned to this website by going to **Files | Properties** of the site and clicking on the **Certificates** button, as follows:

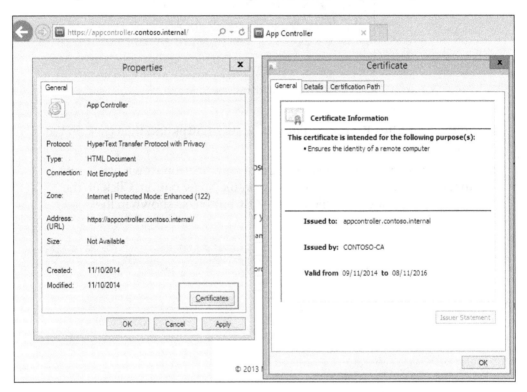

Customizing App Controller branding

In some scenarios corporate branding is required. It is very simple to change the branding on App Controller management portal pages. The following screenshot highlights the areas that can be changed by altering or replacing specific files on the App Controller server:

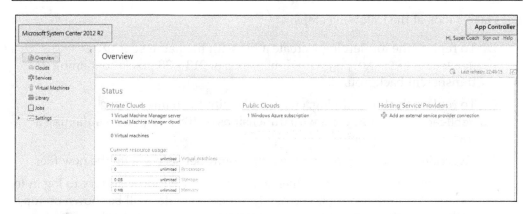

Both files are typically located at C:\Program Files\Microsoft System Center 2012 R2\App Controller\wwwroot, as shown in the following screenshot:

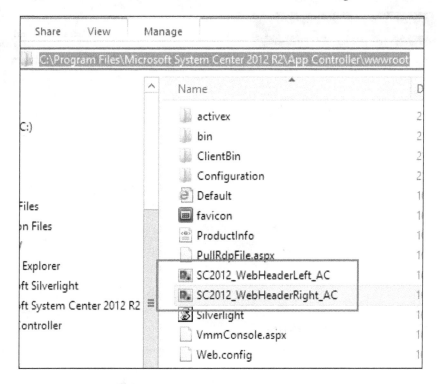

Let's take a look at the following steps:

1. To replace the top-left logo, create a file with the name `SC2012_WebHeaderLeft_AC.png` with dimensions of 213 x 38 pixels containing a transparent background.

2. To replace the top-right log, create a file with the name `SC2012_WebHeaderRight_AC.png` with dimensions of 108 x 16 pixels containing a transparent background.

3. Override the existing files on the App Controller server with the new files.

4. Close the browser window. Open a new browser window and try to log in to the App Controller portal. The newly added logo files will be shown on top of the logon dialog box, as shown in the following screenshot:

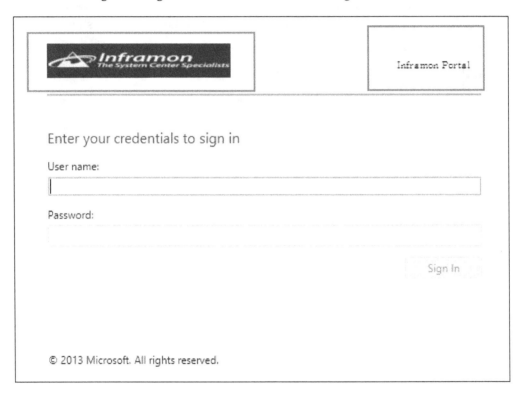

5. The same new branding logos will be displayed after logging on to the App Controller Management portal, as shown in the following screenshot:

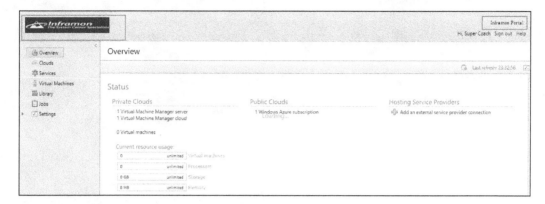

Summary

In this chapter, we integrated Virtual Machine Manager in the App Controller. We also attached a Windows Azure subscription to the App Controller. We added a network share to the App Controller environment and saw how to configure roles-based access users. We also changed the SSL certificate of the App Controller admin portal.

In the next chapter, we will explore advanced features of System Center 2012 R2 App Controller and PowerShell cmdlets that are provided for App Controller.

5
Exploring Advanced Options

In this chapter, we will explore the advanced functionality provided by System Center 2012 R2 App Controller. App Controller gives us the single pane of glass console to administrate the on-premises private cloud and public cloud. We can migrate virtual machines from the on-premises private cloud to the Azure cloud. App Controller also provides a functionality to view operating system images and service templates available in the Azure cloud.

In this chapter, we will cover the following topics:

- Copying VHD files from a private cloud to the Azure cloud
- App Controller PowerShell module installation
- Introduction to App Controller PowerShell cmdlets

In previous chapters, we installed App Controller. For help with App Controller installation, refer to *Chapter 2, Installing and Working with Different App Controller Components*.

Copying VHD files from a private cloud to Microsoft Azure

In this section, we will be copying a virtual machine VHD file to the Azure cloud. Then, we can use the uploaded VHD file during deployment of a virtual machine. We must configure a storage location to upload the VHD file in the Azure cloud. Before we can upload the VHD file, some limitations need to be kept in mind during the preparation of the file, which are as follows:

- At the time of writing this, the Azure cloud supports the following Windows operating systems: Windows Server 2008 R2, Windows Server 2012, and Windows Server 2012 R2.

- At the time of writing this, the newer VHDX format is not supported in Azure. We can, however, convert VHDX to the VHD format using Hyper-V manager. We can also use the `convert-vhd` PowerShell integrated cmdlet. If you get an error message for `convert-vhd` cmdlet not found, then add Remote Server Administration Tools and Hyper-V Module for Windows PowerShell in the server manager. The Hyper-V role is also required for successful conversion.

- Remote desktop must be enabled on the virtual machine.

- Do not Sysprep the virtual machine, instead simply shutdown the virtual machine. If you are preparing to upload VHD with a custom image to the Azure gallery, then Sysprep is required.

- A local administrative user account and password must be set on the virtual machine.

To complete the tasks mentioned in the previous points, perform the following steps:

1. VHD upload steps will be performed mostly in the App Controller console.

2. Now, we will create a location in the Azure cloud to store our VHD file. Log on to the **App Controller** console and select **Library** from the left pane. Now, select the **Windows Azure** section in the middle pane and expand **Azure Demo Environment**. Ensure that **Azure Demo Environment** is selected and click on **Create Storage Account** in the top menu, as shown in the following screenshot:

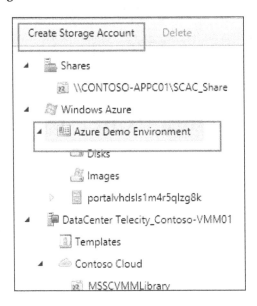

3. Provide a unique name and region in the settings. Click on the **OK** button. I have provided `azurestoragedemoacc01` as the name. In the next couple of minutes, a new storage account will show up in the App Controller console.

4. Select the new `azurestoragedemoacc01` storage account and click on the **Create Container** button in the top menu. Name it `vhds` and click on the **OK** button.

5. We can also use the Windows PowerShell module for App Controller to perform these tasks. Use **Import-module AppController** and get **command-module AppController** to see all 29 cmdlets available for App Controller.

6. Use the following script in PowerShell ISE to connect to the App Controller server:

```
Import-Module AppController
$cred= 'get-credential'
$scac= 'https://appcontroller.contoso.internal'
Get-SCACServer -ServerName $scac -Credential $cred
```

7. In the **App Controller** console, click on the **Library** link in the left pane. From the middle pane, expand the private cloud created in the VMM server by clicking on the triangle to the left of the name. Select the on-premises private cloud library `MSSCVMMLibrary`. A list of available content in the library will be displayed in the right pane. Right-click on the required VHD file in the right pane and select **Copy**. Then browse to `SCAC_Share`, created earlier in the Adding a network share section in *Chapter 4, Customizing App Controller*. Right-click on an empty area in the right pane and select **Paste**. Take a look at the following screenshot:

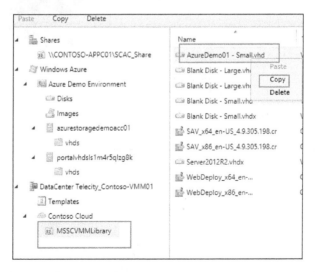

8. Select the \SCAC_Share file that we created earlier from the middle pane. Right-click on the right pane and select **Paste**. For instructions on creating a share, refer to the *Adding a network share* section in *Chapter 4, Customizing App Controller*.

9. Now right-click on the VHD file from SCAC_Share area, and select the **Copy** option as shown in the following screenshot:

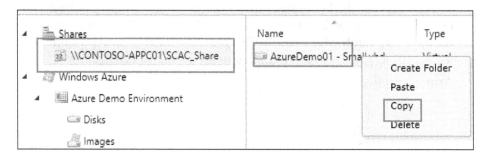

10. From the middle pane, select **Windows Azure** and the **azurestoragedemoacc01** storage account. Expand and select the vhds container. Right-click on the right pane and select the **Paste** option, as shown in the following screenshot:

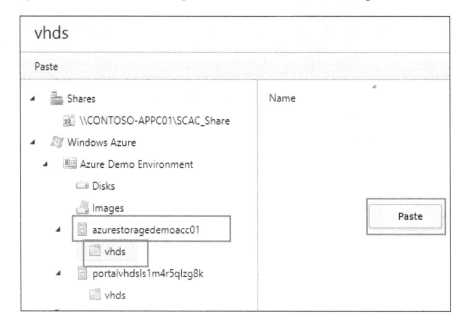

11. Once the VHD file upload job has finished, the uploaded file will show up in the right pane, as shown in the following screenshot:

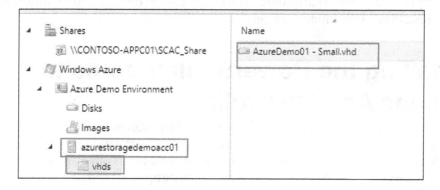

12. We can also verify a successful upload by logging on to **Azure Management Portal** and browsing to the **Storage** account name. Then, selecting **Containers** tab in the dashboard followed by selecting the **vhds** container, as shown in the following screenshot:

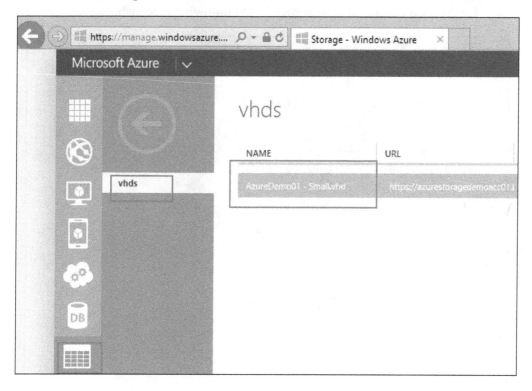

13. Now, we can use this VHD file during deployment of a new virtual machine in the Azure cloud. We can also create an image file from the VHD files uploaded to the Azure cloud. The image can be used to deploy multiple instances in the cloud services.

Installing the PowerShell module to manage App Controller

In this section, we will install the App Controller PowerShell module as a separate component to a virtual machine. The idea behind this installation is to provide specialized cmdlets to manage App Controller on a machine other than the App Controller server. The following steps walk you through this task:

1. Log on to the machine that requires the module. Copy the App Controller installation media or attach the installation **ISO** media.

2. Right-click on `Setup.exe` and select **Run as administrator**. Once the App Controller setup launches, select the **Install Windows PowerShell module for App Controller** link, as shown in the following screenshot:

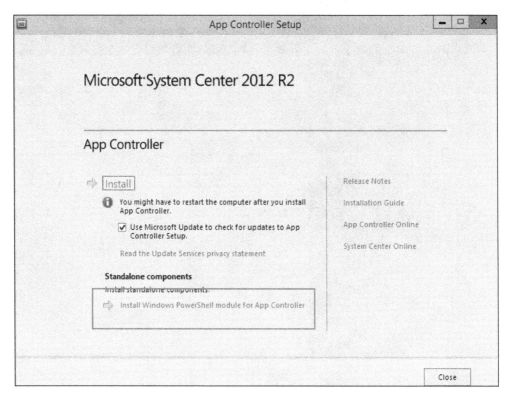

3. On the **Windows PowerShell module for App Controller setup** wizard dialog box, click on **Next**.

4. Accept the license agreement and click on **Next**.

5. On the **Destination Folder** dialog page, change the installation path if required and click on **Next**, as shown in the following screenshot:

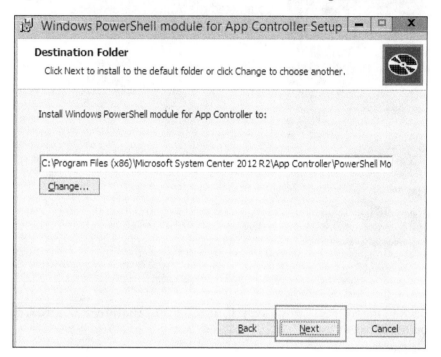

6. On the **Ready to install** dialog page, click on **Install**.

7. On the **Completed Windows PowerShell module for App Controller setup** wizard, click on **Finish**, as shown in the following screenshot:

8. Back in the **System Center App Controller installation** dialog box, click on the **Close** button.

Introduction to App Controller PowerShell cmdlets

PowerShell enables IT professionals to perform repetitive tasks reliably. Also, there are certain features in the Azure cloud that can only be configured with PowerShell. In this section, we will be introduced to the App Controller PowerShell module.

App Controller PowerShell module provides 29 commands that can be used in the session. In a normal PowerShell console, we can import the cmdlets by importing the App Controller module. This can be achieved by typing the following code in the PowerShell command prompt:

```
Import-Module AppController
```

To get the list of commands available in the App Controller module, type the following command in the PowerShell console:

```
Get-Command -Module AppController
```

The following screenshot shows the App Controller module:

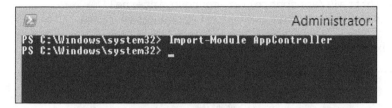

The following commands are available to be used in the App Controller module:

Name	Module
Add-SCACAzureDisk	AppController
Add-SCACAzureImage	AppController
Add-SCACAzureSubscription	AppController
Add-SCACCloudSystem	AppController
Add-SCACShare	AppController
Export-SCACAesKey	AppController
Get-SCACAdminSetting	AppController
Get-SCACAzureHostedService	AppController
Get-SCACAzureRoleInstance	AppController
Get-SCACAzureServiceDeployment	AppController
Get-SCACAzureSubscription	AppController
Get-SCACCloudSystem	AppController
Get-SCACJob	AppController
Get-SCACServer	AppController
Get-SCACShare	AppController
Get-SCACTemporaryStorage	AppController
Get-SCACUserRole	AppController
New-SCACUserRole	AppController
New-SCACUserRoleScope	AppController
Remove-SCACAzureSubscription	AppController
Remove-SCACCloudSystem	AppController
Remove-SCACShare	AppController
Remove-SCACUserRole	AppController
Resume-SCACServiceDeployment	AppController
Set-SCACAdminSetting	AppController
Set-SCACCloudSystem	AppController
Set-SCACTemporaryStorage	AppController
Set-SCACUserRole	AppController
Suspend-SCACServiceDeployment	AppController

We also have the ability to connect to the App Controller server under the context of the permission allowed to a specific user. Launch PowerShell ISE as an administrator and run the following script:

```
Import-Module AppController
$cred= Get-credential
$scac= 'https://appcontroller.contoso.internal'
Get-SCACServer -ServerName $scac -Credential $cred
```

A dialog box as shown in the following screenshot appears:

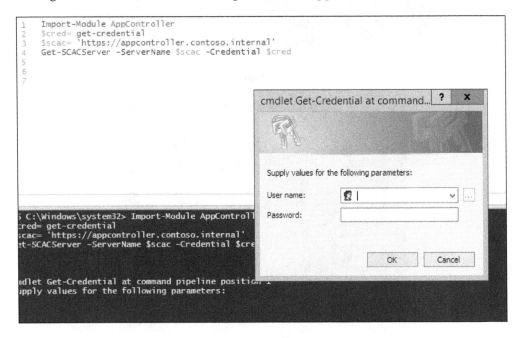

The previous script will pop up a credential dialog for authentication. Once authenticated, all the commands that run against the App Controller server will allow an access level configured for the credentials provided. Please replace the value for $SCAC according to your App Controller environment.

Displaying the App Controller shares in PowerShell

Launch PowerShell for App Controller by searching for applications and typing PowerShell. Right-click and run as administrator. After the console launches, type the following command:

```
Get-SCACShare
```

The following path will be displayed:

The previous command will show all the App Controller shares attached to the connected server.

Installing the Windows Azure PowerShell

In this section, we will introduce Windows Azure PowerShell. PowerShell is very good at performing repetitive tasks and most of the time tasks that cannot be performed from the GUI. The following procedure walks you through the steps for installation:

1. Download the **Microsoft Azure PowerShell** module. At the time of writing this, the module version is 0.8.11 release date 0.0.11. Microsoft Azure PowerShell web installer can be obtained from `http://go.microsoft.com/fwlink/p/?linkid=320376&clcid=0x409`.

2. Once the installer is downloaded, select **Run as administrator**. Accept EULA and click on the download button on the Web Platform Installer 5.0 setup wizard. Once the prerequisite software has been downloaded and installed successfully, click on **Exit**.

3. Search for **Azure PowerShell**. Right-click on the **Microsoft Azure PowerShell** application and select **Run as administrator**, as shown in the following screenshot:

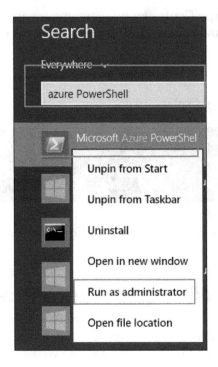

4. Connect to your **Azure Subscription** via PowerShell. Type the Get-AzurePublishSettingsFile command. This will open a browser window for authentication.

5. After the authentication, download the settings file. Now, back in PowerShell console, type Import-AzurePublishSettingsFile -PublishSettingsFile 'C:\Media\azuresettings.publishsettings'. Here, we saved the settings file as Azure settings.

6. Confirm the Azure connection by typing the Get-Azure Subscription command. This will show details about the current subscription.

Summary

In this chapter, we looked into advanced features enabled by App Controller. We covered the migration of a virtual machine VHD file to the Azure cloud, creation of a new storage account in the Azure cloud, installation of the App Controller PowerShell module on a remote machine, connecting PowerShell to Azure subscription, and also the Windows Azure module.

In the next chapter, we will be looking into disaster recovery options available for App Controller.

6
Backup and Recovery

In this chapter, we will discuss the procedure to backup System Center 2012 R2 App Controller. The App Controller server itself is database agnostic meaning as long as we have a good backup copy of the App Controller database. A new App Controller server can be installed using the recovered database and backed up encryption key during the setup process.

In this chapter, we will cover the following points:

- Performing a backup of the App Controller database
- Making disaster recovery planning decisions for App Controller recovery
- Recovering App Controller service from backup

Available choices

As mentioned previously, the App Controller server when deployed with a remote SQL Server does not contain a lot of information. This gives us a lot of choices for planning a backup of the App Controller environment. We can use multiple methods to perform a backup of the App Controller environment, as follows:

- Using traditional tools such as SQL Server Management Studio to perform database backup and using Windows Backup to perform system state backup of the operating system.
- Using System Center 2012 R2 Data Protection Manager to perform scheduled backup of the App Controller SQL database and **BMR (bare metal recovery)** of the operating system running App Controller binaries.

- Restoring App Controller database to an existing environment without running an App Controller setup by backing up the App Controller database only using traditional or enterprise-level backup tools. During disaster recovery, install App Controller as a fresh install. Then restore the previously backed up App Controller database to the newly deployed environment, taking into account that the service pack or feature pack versions are the same.

Procedure

In this section, we will describe the backup and recovery procedure. To perform a successful recovery during backup, the App Controller **advanced encryption standard (AES)** key must be exported by performing the following steps:

1. Launch PowerShell ISE as an administrator on the App Controller server.

2. Run the following script, replacing ServerName and Password for the key file according to your requirements:

```
Import-Module AppController
$Credentials = Get-Credential
Get-SCACServer -ServerName 'https://appcontroller.contoso.
internal' -Credential $Credentials
$Password = ConvertTo-SecureString "PassWord01" -AsPlainText
-Force
Export-SCACAESKey -Path "C:\Media\Key.txt" -Password $Password
```

Backing up App Controller

In this section, we will cover the steps required to make a backup of the System Center 2012 R2 App Controller server, as follows:

1. Log on to the App Controller server and launch **Windows PowerShell ISE** as an administrator.

2. Run the following script and change the values of the server URL and
    password according to your environment:

```
Import-Module AppController
$Credentials = Get-Credential
Get-SCACServer -ServerName 'https://appcontroller.contoso.internal' -Credential $Credentials
$Password = ConvertTo-SecureString "PassWord01" -AsPlainText -Force
Export-SCACAESKey -Path "C:\Media\Key.txt" -Password $Password
```

3. Launch SQL Server Management Studio on the SQL server hosting the App
    Controller database. In our case, it is a remote server. Take a look at the
    following screenshot:

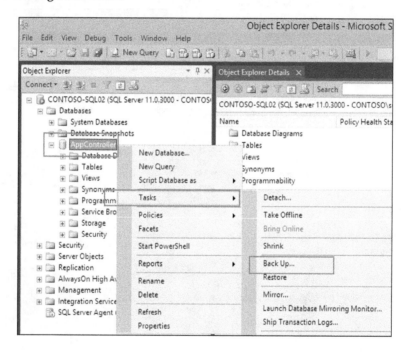

4. In the **Back Up Database** dialog box, specify **Name**, **Description**, and **Destination** to store the backup file. Click on the **Add** button in the destination section as follows:

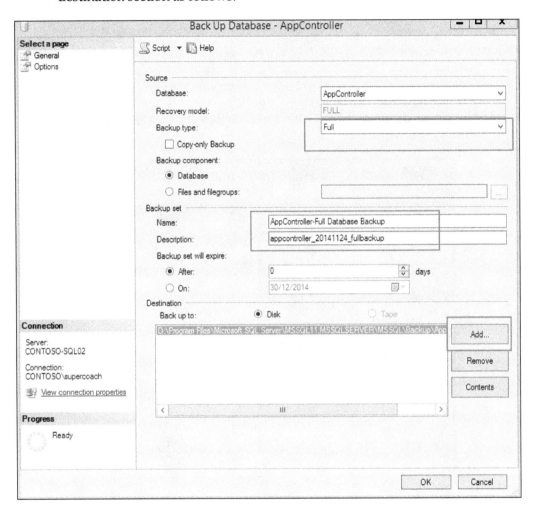

5. In the **Select Backup Destination** dialog box, click on the **...** button next to the **File name** path box, as shown in the following screenshot:

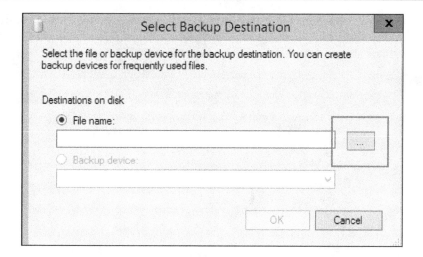

6. In the **Locate Database Files** dialog box, browse to the custom folder that will be used for storing the backup file. Specify the name of the backup file. Then click on the **OK** button as shown in the following screenshot:

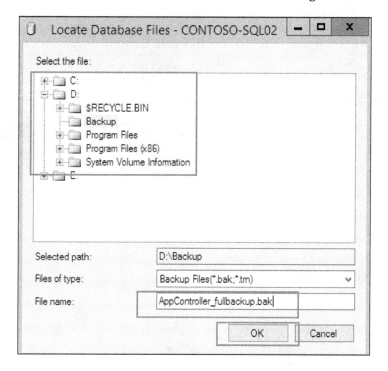

7. In the **Select Backup Destination** dialog box, the specified folder path and filename should be auto-filled in the filename box. Then click on the **OK** button as shown in the following screenshot:

8. Back in the **Back Up Database** dialog box, if any other backup destinations exist in the destination section other than the one we just specified, then select each entry and click on the **Remove** button.

9. Optionally, you can switch to the **Options** tab from the left pane and select the checkbox next to **Verify backup when finished**. Then click on **OK** button as shown in the following screenshot:

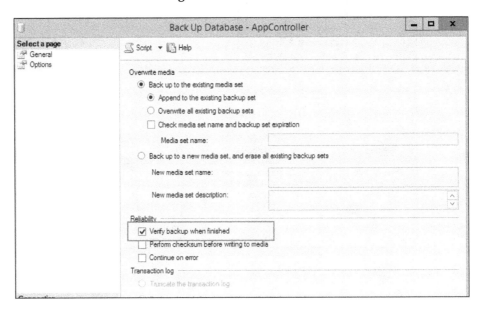

10. Wait for the backup job to finish. Once the job execution completes, a dialog box will pop up. Click on **OK** to close the following dialog box:

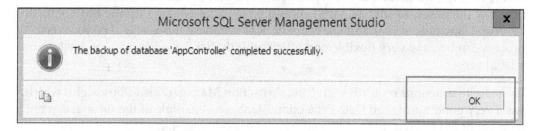

11. To confirm a successful backup, open Windows Explorer and browse to the folder specified earlier in the **Back Up Database** dialog box, as follows:

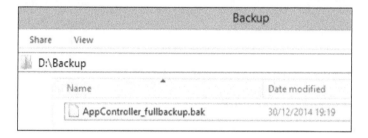

Restoring App Controller

In this section, we will explain the procedure to restore the App Controller service. Let's go through the following points:

1. To restore the App Controller service, use traditional tools such as SQL Server Management Studio to restore the backup copy of the database.

2. Then run the App Controller setup as part of the disaster recovery process; provide the **AES key** file we exported in the previous section during the setup wizard.

Summary

In this chapter, we looked at the type of backups that can be created for disaster recovery purposes. Ideally, SCDPM should be used for backing up the BMR state of the App Controller server and snapshot of SQL database if possible. The recovery process can become very flexible and efficient with disk-based short term backup on a DPM server.

For more instructions on BMR with Data Protection Manager, visit Pluralsight, which has a very good tutorial on Data Protection Manager. A sample of the tutorial can be found at `http://blog.pluralsight.com/videos/scdpm-bare-metal-recovery`.

This concludes the *Learning System Center App Controller* book by *Packt Publishing*. We hope you have enjoyed this book as much as we enjoyed writing it.

Index

Thank you for buying
Learning System Center App Controller

About Packt Publishing

Packt, pronounced 'packed', published its first book, *Mastering phpMyAdmin for Effective MySQL Management*, in April 2004, and subsequently continued to specialize in publishing highly focused books on specific technologies and solutions.

Our books and publications share the experiences of your fellow IT professionals in adapting and customizing today's systems, applications, and frameworks. Our solution-based books give you the knowledge and power to customize the software and technologies you're using to get the job done. Packt books are more specific and less general than the IT books you have seen in the past. Our unique business model allows us to bring you more focused information, giving you more of what you need to know, and less of what you don't.

Packt is a modern yet unique publishing company that focuses on producing quality, cutting-edge books for communities of developers, administrators, and newbies alike. For more information, please visit our website at www.packtpub.com.

About Packt Enterprise

In 2010, Packt launched two new brands, Packt Enterprise and Packt Open Source, in order to continue its focus on specialization. This book is part of the Packt Enterprise brand, home to books published on enterprise software – software created by major vendors, including (but not limited to) IBM, Microsoft, and Oracle, often for use in other corporations. Its titles will offer information relevant to a range of users of this software, including administrators, developers, architects, and end users.

Writing for Packt

We welcome all inquiries from people who are interested in authoring. Book proposals should be sent to author@packtpub.com. If your book idea is still at an early stage and you would like to discuss it first before writing a formal book proposal, then please contact us; one of our commissioning editors will get in touch with you.

We're not just looking for published authors; if you have strong technical skills but no writing experience, our experienced editors can help you develop a writing career, or simply get some additional reward for your expertise.

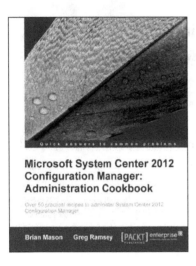

Microsoft System Center 2012 Configuration Manager:

Microsoft System Center 2012 Configuration Manager: Administration Cookbook

Over 50 practical recipes to administer System Center 2012 Configuration Manager

Brian Mason   Greg Ramsey   [PACKT] enterprise

Microsoft System Center 2012 Configuration Manager: Administration Cookbook

ISBN: 978-1-84968-494-1   Paperback: 224 pages

Over 50 practical recipes to administer System Center 2012 Configuration Manager

1. Administer System Center 2012 Configuration Manager.

2. Provides fast answers to questions commonly asked by new administrators.

3. Skip the why's and go straight to the how-to's.

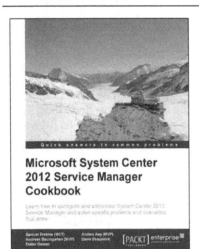

Microsoft System Center 2012 Service Manager Cookbook

Learn how to configure and administer System Center 2012 Service Manager and solve specific problems and scenarios that arise

Samuel Erskine (MCT)   Anders Asp (MVP)
Andreas Baumgarten (MVP)   Steve Beaumont
Dieter Gasser   [PACKT] enterprise

Microsoft System Center 2012 Service Manager Cookbook

ISBN: 978-1-84968-694-5   Paperback: 474 pages

Learn how to configure and administer System Center 2012 Service Manager and solve specific problems and scenarios that arise

1. Practical cookbook with recipes that will help you get the most out of Microsoft System Center 2012 Service Manager.

2. Learn the various methods and best practices administrating and using Microsoft System Center 2012 Service Manager.

Please check **www.PacktPub.com** for information on our titles

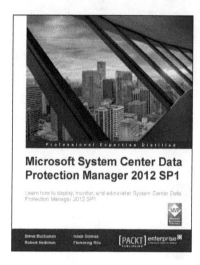

Microsoft System Center Data Protection Manager 2012 SP1

ISBN: 978-1-84968-630-3 Paperback: 328 pages

Learn how to deploy, monitor, and administer System Center Data Protection Manager 2012 SP1

1. Practical guidance that will help you get the most out of Microsoft System Center Data Protection Manager 2012.

2. Gain insight into deploying, monitoring, and administering System Center Data Protection Manager 2012 from a team of Microsoft MVPs.

3. Learn the various methods and best practices for administrating and using Microsoft System Center Data Protection Manager 2012.

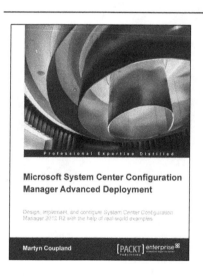

Microsoft System Center Configuration Manager Advanced Deployment

ISBN: 978-1-78217-208-6 Paperback: 290 pages

Design, implement, and configure System Center Configuration Manager 2012 R2 with the help of real-world examples

1. Learn how to design and operate Configuration Manager 2012 R2 sites.

2. Explore the power of Configuration Manager 2012 R2 for managing your client and server estate.

Please check **www.PacktPub.com** for information on our titles